Ben
A Test of Faith

The Ben Klassen Story

By

Sandie Klassen

© 2002 by Sandie Klassen. All rights reserved.

No part of this book may be reproduced, stored in a retrieval system, or transmitted by any means, electronic, mechanical, photocopying, recording, or otherwise, without written permission from the author.

ISBN: 1-4033-8963-2 (e-book)
ISBN: 1-4033-8964-0 (Paperback)
ISBN: 1-4033-8965-9 (Dustjacket)

Library of Congress Control Number: 2002095446

This book is printed on acid free paper.

Printed in the United States of America
Bloomington, IN

Editor: Carol Light
Cover Photo: Tonya Malay

1stBooks - rev. 11/20/02

This book describes the author's experience while having her son treated for cancer and reflects her opinions relating to those experiences. Some names and identifying details of individuals mentioned in the book have been changed to protect their privacy.

In Memory of My Wonderful Mom, Betty

Dedicated to My Precious Daughter, Dana

CONTENTS

Acknowledgments ix
1. Blue Skies to Gray 1
2. The Start of a Journey 10
3. The Diagnosis 16
4. What Now? 23
5. The Drive Back 28
6. Admitted 32
7. What Is It? 40
8. Taking Pictures 45
9. The Protocol 52
10. Germs 61
11. Choosing Duke 72
12. The Central Line 81
13. Harvesting 90
14. One Last Dose 98
15. Our Farewell 103
16. Apartment Life 122
17. Our First Day at Duke 130
18. Radiation 133
19. The Green Mask 143
20. Packing 146
21. The Unit 152
22. Pre-Transplant 157
23. 96 Hours of Destruction 161
24. A Very Sick Boy 163
25. Transplant Day 172
26. Grow Cells Grow 179
27. Just Keep Waiting 189
28. Pepperoni Pizza 198
29. Home Away From Home 203
30. Rainbows 210
31. Going In Style 214
Epilogue 218

ACKNOWLEDGMENTS

I started this project by sitting down to write "Thank You" notes to all of the people who knowingly and unknowingly helped us through this most difficult journey. I spent hours trying to come up with the words that would most accurately express just how grateful I am to each person, and exactly when their cards, calls, prayers, visits and gifts helped the most. The list of people I want to thank is probably longer than this book, but to each and every one of you, I want to say "thank you".

This book tells our story from the day Benjamin was diagnosed with cancer until his one-year anniversary after transplant. It certainly is not a scholarly piece of work but it is from my heart. I share with you intimate feelings and experiences because I want you to know how involved you really were in our recovery. I tried to make this story as detailed as possible because I wanted you to actually live each moment again with us. Also, when Ben is a grown man and is interested in knowing more about his early childhood, I wanted it to be clearly written for him. I've dedicated this book to my daughter Dana because I love her more than life itself and am so proud of who she is, but I am also dedicating it to you. I cannot Thank You enough for caring about us, cooking for us, and mostly, for praying for us. We truly could not have made it without your help. This book is a thank you to all of you, so…THANK YOU from the bottom of my heart!

Whenever I read a book, I always glance at the 'acknowledgment' section, but I usually just skim over the page. I realize now however, just how important these people are to the author, so I must add my list of special people too. To my loving husband Chuck. To my Dad. To Vonita, Lee, and all of my immediate and extended family. To Miss Patty, Lisa, Larry, and Bobbie. To Mrs. Bunge our BUMBEE, Amy Evola, Laura Koch, and to Bonnie Craven, Robin Gehrke, Rick Carlton, Berta Hinton and Debbie Greenwood. To the entire team at The Children's Hospital in Ft. Myers, Florida and especially to Dr. Salman and Debbie White. To the great staff at Duke. To every single person at the family of Hope Lutheran Church. To Erinn Hutkin, to all our employees and to all of the people of our community. To everyone who sent a card and an e-mail. And most of all to Jesus. Thank you for giving Benjamin a chance at life.

Love,
Sandie

1

Blue Skies to Gray

I typically loved Fridays, and it seemed as if this one was going to be nothing but another terrific day. The long week of work had gone very well, and life in general was absolutely perfect. Although I thoroughly enjoyed my work as a physical therapist and the time I spent at my career, I was especially fond of Fridays because, like most people, my husband Chuck and I had two days off to spend in a different environment than the office. We loved having the free time to be together with our two children as a family, sharing each other's company and doing fun activities.

This particular December Friday seemed unusually special because we had a great weekend of events planned, and it looked as if the weather was going to cooperate. The sky was its usual magnificent blue, the temperature was a perfect seventy-five degrees, and the feeling in the air was light and fresh. We lived in Bonita Springs, a small but rapidly growing community nestled between Ft. Myers and Naples on the west coast of Florida. When I walked outside to get the morning newspaper, I paused in the driveway for a moment and looked up into the incredibly clear, cloudless sky. I stood tall, smiled, and filled my lungs to capacity with the pure, clean air. I loved Southwest Florida winters. The sun was not quite as intense as in the summer, and there was rarely any humidity. I drew in another happy breath and picked up the newspaper.

That Friday started like any other morning for our family. We were in great moods and were excited about a new day. Our children, Benjamin and Dana, scampered happily through the house as we went about our normal routine to get ready for work and prepare for Miss Patty, our nanny, to arrive. Ben, who was three years old, decided that he wanted to make French toast for breakfast, which was of no surprise to me. It was one of his favorites, and his usual breakfast request. I think it was a favorite food mostly because his job was to crack open the eggs for me and then to dip the Wonder Bread into the mixture. We fixed it together, and soon the French toast was sprinkled with cinnamon, and the fresh Florida orange juice was poured into the usual three-inch high blue and green plastic cups. Chuck, my husband of eight years, had finished his coffee and oatmeal earlier, so he was busy showering and dressing while the children and I ate our breakfast at the kitchen table.

We talked all about our plans for the day, and I could see that the children were as excited about the weekend as I was.

"Do you and Daddy have to go to work today?" Ben asked.

"Yes, but guess what day tomorrow is?" I answered.

Ben immediately started singing the Barney song: "There are seven days, there are seven days, there are seven days in a week…"

I loved when he sang, which was often. When Ben finished his song, I asked, "So, what day is tomorrow?"

He looked at me and grinned. "Tomorrow is Saturday, Mommy, and that is the day you and Daddy get to stay home from work to play with me and Dana." He was excited as he began telling me about all the things he wanted to do together.

Putt-putt golf, as always, was on Ben's agenda. Putt-putt was usually ok with Chuck and me because we managed to complete the eighteen holes at the Golf Safari course in about twenty minutes. "Next hole" was how we rushed through the course. Ben hardly had a chance to finish putting his ball into the cup when one of us would holler, "Next hole!" It kept the game moving quickly past the African animals featured on the course.

Dana, only seven months old, was content to watch the game from her stroller for only a brief time, as she preferred to be part of the real action. Dana was a wonderful addition to our family and a perfect daughter. Ben loved being her big brother. If Dana had her way, she would have been crawling all over the miniature golf course, so we had to keep the game moving. Ben, though, had a passion for putt-putt golf from an early age and even at seven months old would never have sat as contently on the sidelines as his sister.

Benjamin loved all sports. You name the sport, and he wanted to be a part of the game. His bedroom closely resembled an athletic store with its posters and banners hung on the walls and ball caps lined neatly on a shelf. Baseball bats, hockey sticks, and a tennis racquet stood upright in a corner. Of all sports, hockey most peaked his interest, and the breakfast table conversation on that Friday morning soon turned to the Florida Everblades hockey team. They were in town all weekend for a tournament.

"Do you think the Everblades will score, Mommy?" asked Ben.

"Oh, I bet they will," I answered.

"I do, too. I think they are the best team in the whole wide world," Ben said in a matter-of-fact tone. "Can we get some pizza before the game?"

"Sure," I said, not really thinking much about dinner. I was helping Dana dip her French toast into her syrup "dipping pond."

We had plans to go to dinner and then to the Friday evening hockey game. Ben had decided to wear his new jersey and had already asked if he could bring along the puck that the usher had given to him two weeks earlier. The puck was stored in our freezer at Ben's insistence because that was what the "real" hockey players did. On Saturday, after our putt-putt golf outing, we were going to be off to another hockey event at TECO Arena in Ft. Myers. Our weekends were always busy like this because we loved to pack the day with family activities. Just being together was very satisfying for us.

And so we finished breakfast, and soon Chuck and I were off to work. The only addition to our usual Friday routine was Ben's doctor's appointment. We didn't know then that visiting the doctor for a checkup would turn this beautiful, clear, sunny Friday into a giant, dark storm that would change our lives forever.

■■■

I left the office at 10:35 a.m., already late. I had hoped to tear myself away from my desk by 10:15 so that I would have ample time to go home to pick up Ben and take him to the pediatrician's office for his 11:00 a.m. appointment. But, as usual, I was late, so I raced out of the office parking lot, drove about two miles north, and then turned left into the entrance of our subdivision. I impatiently waited for the guardhouse attendant to raise the gate so that I could make my way into the community and to our house. I mumbled to myself, "Come on, come on." As soon as the gate rose, I waved and then pressed the gas pedal until I was doing nearly 40 mph. The speed limit was only 25 mph; and I always drove too fast on this entrance road.

Everything in my life was done at lightning speed. I've always been that way, and Ben was just like me. We loved the kiddie roller coasters and fast boats. I was surprised that I didn't get a ticket for speeding that day because I certainly deserved one. As always, I should have left the office just a few minutes earlier and given myself plenty of time to go where I needed to be without being pressed by the clock. Why did I always have to be in such a rush? I wondered. If I'd left just ten minutes earlier, I could have enjoyed a nice leisurely trip.

"Oh," I sighed aloud, "someday I won't be in such a hurry, and then I'll slow down to enjoy the simple things in life."

We made it safely to the pediatrician's office in Bonita Springs, a smaller, more simplified facility that was a branch to his primary medical practice in Fort Myers. I was relieved to see that we were only about four minutes late for our scheduled appointment. I signed Ben's name onto the sign-in sheet at the counter, smiled and nodded to the girl on the phone behind the closed glass window, and took a seat in the "well kids" section. It's funny how they put the well kids section in the back of the waiting room so that you have to walk past all of the coughing, sneezing, sick kids to get to your "healthy" seat. Ben and I walked past several sick children. I was trying to hold my breath, hoping that Ben was holding his breath, too, so that we would not catch a cold or flu virus that might ruin our weekend plans.

We took our seats and waited ten minutes for a nurse to call us back to an examination room. Ben played happily with the only toy in the room, a tabletop arrangement constructed of wood and metal. The toy looked more like a piece of modern art with its many contorted, colored pieces of metal twisting in all directions from a wooden base. The object for the child playing was to move a small train of round balls up, down, over, under, and all along the pieces of metal coated in red, blue, yellow, and green paint. It really was creative and probably had some fancy developmental purpose behind it, but to Ben it just looked fun.

As he played quietly, I studied the bruises on his legs and the pale color of his skin. I had been worried about these bruises because they seemed to develop so frequently lately, and they appeared after even the slightest bump. Something was just not normal about them. We had recently returned from a hiking trip up in the mountains of New Hampshire, so I concluded that the bruises on his shins were from his

A Test of Faith

short little legs bumping into tree roots on the rugged path of the Appalachian Trail.

He also complained about his feet hurting on that trip, but again I thought I had a reasonable explanation: Ben seemed to be going through a growth spurt. Most of his pants were now about one inch too short, and I supposed that his shoes were probably just too small as well. Not a problem, I thought. We would need to purchase new shoes as soon as we returned home. When the new shoes did not make any difference in his foot pain, I started to worry. My worry intensified when he also began to complain of a headache. The new complaint of pain in his forehead had started at breakfast on Wednesday, so I immediately made the doctor's appointment, which was scheduled for today, Friday, December 8, 2000.

Sitting in the pediatrician's office, I realized that I was terribly worried about Ben and had been for about three or four days. I guess something can be said about a mother's instinct. I tried desperately to suppress my gut feeling that something serious was wrong and hoped with all my might that this would just turn out to be a routine checkup. Possibly, I thought, the doctor would make a recommendation for some iron supplements to resolve this newly acquired bruising tendency.

When Ben's name was called, we were led into an office equipped with the basics, which included a small countertop centrifuge used to spin the drop of blood they took from Ben's right index finger. The doctor himself actually did the finger stick, which surprised me. As he swiped Ben's fingertip with an alcohol-soaked cotton ball, I tried to explain my concerns.

"You see, Doctor, these bruises just do not seem normal." I told him. "I feel something is wrong."

The doctor nodded at my comments, and I thought I noticed a slight shrug of his shoulder. "You mothers are always overreacting," he said as he pricked Ben.

I could feel the heat of my anger building. The sudden warmth of intense emotion burned my ears. I had spent eight years studying at university level to earn two Master of Science degrees. I had met and succeeded the challenge of a year of medical school courses to earn a degree in physical therapy. Although I was no physician, I had accumulated a fair amount of medical knowledge in ten years of practicing PT, and I certainly was not a wishy-washy and "overreacting" mother.

The doctor ignored me while he collected a thin tube of Ben's blood. When the tube was ready, the doctor left the room, and Ben and I once again sat alone, waiting.

When the doctor returned, he said that he was sure the machine was acting up, so he again started his routine of poking another of Ben's fingers. This time when he left the room, he made the mistake of leaving a first-year resident alone with us.

"Something is wrong with this little boy," I said firmly to the young, green physician. "Will you please examine him or tell that doctor friend of yours to listen seriously to me?"

The young resident, who I'm not sure shaved yet, replied, "Okay, let's see."

He began to do a very impressive abdominal examination of Ben's belly. He asked me detailed questions about the bruises and the complaints of pain that Ben had reported to me earlier in the week. He looked into Ben's mouth, eyes, and ears. He did not stop looking at Ben or concentrating on my questions until the older, seemingly disinterested doctor reappeared. Then the young resident stood tall and faced the senior doctor. His eyes had a determined glint.

"Sir, I believe this mother has some valid concerns. I think we should hear her out, Doctor."

The older, more experienced man paid little attention to the resident. Instead, he turned to me and said, "I have some concerns about Benjamin's blood work, but I'm not sure if I am getting an accurate reading from my machine, or if there is something wrong."

"What could be wrong?" I asked.

He didn't answer my question. Instead, he handed me a piece of paper with a name and phone number on it. "Please take your son to see this doctor. There's no other way to test blood here in this facility, so I'd like for you to have Ben tested by Dr. Salman at Healthpark Hospital in Ft. Myers. Mrs. Klassen, your son's blood count is severely abnormal. It's best to obtain a second opinion in case my equipment is malfunctioning."

I looked down at the paper and read the scribbled name and number. I had no idea what type of medicine Dr. Salman practiced, but something about the pediatrician's look when he handed me the paper made me nervous. He was very stoic and matter-of-fact in his demeanor, which was not anything new for that visit; however, there was something different in his eyes. He seemed hesitant and withdrawn, as if he were burdened by a heavy sadness and was attempting to keep an emotional distance from Ben and me. He appeared to be doing a good job of not caring, and I was mad.

I was teetering on rude when I looked the man in the eyes and said, "I sure hope this Dr. Salman has more interest in my baby than you obviously do." I then turned to the younger doctor and said, "Thank you so much, Doctor. You were incredible and will be very successful as a pediatrician. Thank you."

The stuffy older doctor just looked at me, speechless. I walked past him holding Benjamin and said nothing more.

I learned later that Ben's hemoglobin count at that initial doctor's visit was 6.1 when it should have been around 12.0, and his platelets were 15 but were supposed to be 150. Medically, Ben was in serious condition.

I drove from the pediatrician's office back to the physical therapy clinic that Chuck and I owned and operated. I drove slowly and patiently. I was never more responsible and cautious in my driving and never more pleased to be stuck behind a slow moving, sightseeing tourist. I was stopped by every red light and was content with that, too. I was not able to function any faster and felt a desperate need to move at a snail's pace. I also needed some time to calm my anger and to reflect on the pediatrician's words and what might be wrong with Ben. It seemed as though everything was moving in slow motion and that the world around me was nothing but a Hollywood set. I felt as if I was on the outside looking in onto everything, and everyone was acting a theatrical part.

Ben was his usual happy and bubbly self. He was buckled into his car seat in the back where he always rode and sang a soft tune to himself. I watched him in the rearview mirror for a few seconds and then finally spoke.

"How are you feeling, Ben?"

"Good, Mommy. I'm just a little tired. I think I'll take a nap while we drive to get Dad."

I had already told Ben that we were going to the clinic to tell Chuck what was going on and that we were going to Ft. Myers to see this man named Dr. Salman. I was hoping more than anything that Chuck would go with us. Although I considered myself to be a strong, capable person who felt comfortable taking on most challenges independently, deep down I was afraid to go alone. As I look back, I wonder why I ever questioned that Chuck would go to the Ft. Myers doctor's appointment with us. After all, we were a close family who stuck together in easy times and tough ones. A strong intuitive feeling made me sense that this could turn out to be a really tough time. Maybe that's why I suddenly realized that I needed my husband more than ever.

Chuck was sitting at his desk concentrating on his work when Ben and I walked into the clinic. "Hey, Bud, how was the doctor?" he asked.

"Fine, Dad. No problem," Ben replied lightheartedly.

Then my husband looked at me. I must have been as white and pale as our son because Chuck took me aside to talk while Ben visited with the girls in the front office. Ben loved to go to the clinic to see all the gang. He had known many of them since he was only six weeks old and felt very comfortable giving them hugs, telling stories, and of course, playing sports. Before Chuck and I could start our conversation, Ben already had recruited one of the girls for a game of golf. He had a plastic yellow club that was stored beneath my desk and a wad of tape that one of the fellows had made for him more than a year ago that served as a golf ball. He played with as much energy and enthusiasm as would be expected from any healthy three-year-old boy.

When we finally were able to talk privately, I told Chuck that something frightening was happening and that we had to get a physical exam and some repeat blood work in Ft. Myers at another doctor's office. I told Chuck that the pediatrician had already called Dr. Salman at Healthpark Hospital and that we were supposed to go to his office as soon as possible.

"So what's going on?" Chuck asked. "Why are you in such a hurry?"

I tried to explain but the urgency in my voice and body language only confused him.

"Stop," he said. "Slow down, Sandie. Tell me everything and start at the beginning. I want to know exactly what was said and by whom in that doctor's office."

So I told him. I went through every "he said" and "I said" of the conversation with the pediatricians so that Chuck could completely understand what had happened at the doctor's office and feel as if he had been part of that original conversation himself. He was as mad as a swatted hornet when I told him of the pediatrician's attitude, but he put that emotion aside when I mentioned the abnormal blood count. When I finished talking, he stood quietly, and I guessed that he was trying to rationalize Ben's situation.

After a long inspiration of air and a very slow exhale, Chuck simply said, "Let's go." He put down the file he was holding and his pen, and he locked the office door behind us. Neither of us noticed that the computer in the office was left on and so were the lights.

Before I knew it, we were buckling Ben in the car to head north to Healthpark Hospital as ordered.

2

The Start of a Journey

Dr. Salman's office was indeed at Healthpark Hospital about twenty miles from our home. When we walked through the front doors of the hospital, I was reminded of a lobby of a very fine hotel. I had been to this medical center before because it was where Ben and Dana were both born, and it was the facility that I used for my annual health checkups. I never grew tired of the atrium. There was a river of gently flowing water with bridges. The lush greenery was landscaped to perfection. The coffee shop always emitted the scent of a freshly brewed, flavored coffee, which instantly relaxed me. The usual antiseptic smell of a hospital was nowhere.

In the heart of the atrium, an ebony grand piano played soft background music. On Thursdays, a very slight old woman played the piano. I talked to her once and discovered that she had played many concerts at Carnegie Hall during her prime. She was very talented, and everyone relished her beautiful presentation of the classics. Today, however, no one sat at the piano; it was coming to life via a CD and "pianomation" technology.

The hospital atrium was usually a luxurious and easy place to be. Normally there was a leisurely pace and absolutely no hustle or bustle in the lobby. People moved through it as they would a fine art gallery, but on this day I frantically hurried along. I was incredibly anxious about seeing the doctor.

The old man reading his newspaper at the reception desk looked up over his reading glasses to direct us to our appointment. "Just around that corner," he said, after I requested directions to The Children's Hospital. I'll never forget that moment because when the man pointed toward the hall we were to take, there, in bold large letters mounted on the wall, read "The Children's Hospital, Hematology/Oncology Center. Dr. Salman: Hematology and Oncology."

My heart raced and my mouth grew instantly dry. I looked over at Chuck who was meandering along while holding Ben's hand. He was searching his pocket for a penny as Ben begged to be allowed to throw the coin into the artificial stream.

"Come on you guys, let's go," I said. I sounded as rushed and anxious as I felt. My fears were peaked and my patience was exhausted.

The last time I had an encounter with a hematologist/oncologist had been about two years earlier when my mom was having some calf pain and felt tired all the time. When her general practitioner referred her to a specialist, my dad and I went along, but again, I did not think much about the symptoms except that maybe she needed a vitamin B-12 shot or iron supplements, and that she probably overdid it on the golf course. Iron deficiency ran in our family, and several aunts and uncles received monthly vitamin B-12 injections. We later learned, after weeks of studies and hundreds of tests, that she was not anemic at all. She had pancreatic cancer that had already reached stage four and was completely overtaking her liver.

My mom died about three months later, and I was devastated. She was only fifty-four years old and had just moved to Florida with Dad to retire. Retirement meant playing golf, reading great books, polishing up on their passion for cooking, and spending time falling more and more in love with each other without the stresses of work and kids. But then, suddenly, she was gone, and I was empty and lost without her. My dad's bereavement, sorrow, and pain were far more intense than my own; he had unexpectedly lost his best friend and most wonderful companion. Our entire family was filled with sadness and depression over the fact that cancer had attacked Mom and taken her away from us so unfairly and so early in her life and ours. So, when I saw Dr. Salman's medical discipline, the word *hematologist*, which is an expert on the study of blood, was a blur. Instead, I was totally focused on the word *oncologist*, and I was numb.

The waiting room in Dr. Salman's office was a child's play haven. Two connecting rooms off to the side of the main area were constructed with tall, floor-to-ceiling windows for two of the four walls so that the children would be visible at all times from all angles. Inside, the rooms were filled with a giant dollhouse, kid-sized tables and chairs, a full-sized Kidzpace Playstation, and games, toys, crayons, paper—you name it. Ben walked right in and made himself at home. He played and laughed with the other kids and was quite at ease, now that I look back.

Chuck and I sat stiff and upright in the middle of the row of chairs along the wall. We did not speak but instead stared straight ahead at the seventy-five gallon fish tank. The water appeared blue because of the paint on the backside of the aquarium, and the fish were busy swimming around the mounds of artificial coral, rock, and plants. Above us and to our left was a television mounted in the corner of the room. Disney's *Lady and the Tramp* video was playing with the sound turned up. I recognized "The Siamese Cat Song." The "We are Si-a-mese, if you ple-ase" refrain was bothersome to me.

Those cats and that song took me back to when I was about Ben's age and my grandmother had us watch the movie at her house. *The Wonderful World of Disney* was on every Sunday night, so we always planned to eat popcorn, drink Pepsi-Cola out of the eight-pack bottle carton, and watch the TV show. The time together was terrific, and I treasure the memories, even those of watching *Lady and The Tramp*. I liked the movie very well, but I did not particularly like that song because it sounded screechy to me. The song and music elicited almost the same irritating feeling as someone running their fingernails along a chalkboard. I could not tolerate the sounds, so I soon abandoned my stiff, upright posture and sat slumped over with my elbows propped onto my knees and both hands over my ears.

The receptionist brought out a clipboard with a few papers attached to it and handed me a pen. "Hello, Mrs. Klassen. Do you have any insurance?" she asked.

"Yes, we do," I nervously replied.

"May I please see your insurance cards so that I may copy them for Benjamin's file?" she asked with a brief smile.

As Chuck reached into his wallet and handed over our card, I maintained a rather resentful attitude. This will be brief, so don't bother establishing a permanent file on us or anything, I thought to myself in denial that anything was seriously wrong. I somewhat carelessly began to fill in the blanks on the forms. I noticed that my usual clean, legible handwriting looked more like an aged woman's scribble. My "L's" were more like vertical squiggles instead of straight lines, so I began to concentrate to provide all the information correctly and to take this paperwork seriously. Although we surely would not have a long relationship with this office, I knew that this

A Test of Faith

would be a "permanent" file for at least seven years. Seven years is how long a medical office must keep patients' charts even if they were only there for one visit. So I continued filling in the form.

Let's see, "Patient's Name." I had to stop and think. Forever I had always written my name on these pages for routine visits to dentists and doctors. I'd had normal adult medical services that always resulted in reports of perfect health, but now it was Benjamin's information that they needed.

"Birthday." I took in a deep breath when I wrote down my son's birthday. It had only been twenty-six days since he had turned three years old. He was such a sweet, happy boy and so full of energy and life. I could not believe that he had only been with us for three years. It seemed as though he had been a part of our lives forever.

While Chuck was still mesmerized by the easy efforts of the many colored fish swimming before him, I was soon again lost in thought.

I was twenty-eight years old when I finally decided it was time to really think about becoming a mother. My mom had turned out to be my very best friend, and she was such a fantastic mother that I really thought I had a perfect role model for the job. I was scared, though, and so was Chuck. We weren't sure what we wanted to do about our family plan as we were having a great time just the two of us. We had plenty of time to spend at the office to build our careers, time to exercise regularly, and time to take off for movies, the beach, tons of weekend getaways, and all of that DINK (Double Income, No Kids) lifestyle stuff. So, the decision of whether to start a family was on our minds all of the time, and what an important decision it was to make. Would children make our lives richer and more fulfilling? Did God have a purpose for the child that I might bear? What was God's plan for Chuck and me? We wanted all of these questions answered, and we wanted our decision to be the right one, mainly for the sake of the impending children.

After many days and nights of wondering what I should do next with my life, I finally put it all in God's hands. I sat with my Life Application Bible one night and just skimmed through the reference section. "Index to Notes" was the title of the helpful concordance. It was the reference section that I had resorted to many times before for answers to questions in my life. I would turn to this section at the back of my Bible and scan the bold headings until I found a topic that somehow related to my concern or fear or question. The bold listing would lead me to some scripture that would often provide insight into how God himself would handle the problem, which would then send me off into a thinking mode to search for my own answers. The guidance that the Bible gave me when I felt lost, confused, or indifferent about my emotions was a stable foundation for me. I felt that God truly was my Father in Heaven, and I craved His advice; I also trusted and valued His opinion.

During this particular Bible study time, I was drawn to topic headings such as "indecisiveness," "decisions," "parenting," "children," and "faith." I turned to the related scriptures, and as never before, in no uncertain terms, my question was answered. Nothing was left to my own interpretation or translation as I read Exodus 2:2: "... and she became pregnant and gave birth to a son." Before me was the story about the birth of Moses, and there it was printed in bold black and white. The words "pregnant" and "birth" were right before my eyes without any gloss over or hazy metaphor. The words were as clear as day. At that very moment, as never before in my heart, I realized that I would be forever empty and unfulfilled if I did not have children, and it was obvious to me that God had a plan for my children. My decision was made. God told me what His plan was for my life, and now it was my responsibility to follow His plan or dare to stray, disobey, or try to go on my own. The answer to my prayer was that distinct and obvious.

As I sat in bed propped up against my pillow, I slowly looked around the bedroom. I had chills on the back of my neck and up and down my spine. I felt an unusual presence that was comforting but eerily supernatural at the same time as God Himself, plain and simply, revealed to me His will. During all of my years as a young Christian, I had prayed often and hard but had never before experienced what others had called a true and intimate encounter with the Holy Spirit. Sometimes my doubt hindered prayer and I felt as if I was just talking to an empty blue sky, so when it happened, I was incredibly moved and completely awestruck. My faith and wishes about the reality of God had just moved from hope to knowledge. I knew then that it was time to start a family, and Chuck knew it, too.

As I waited for Dr. Salman to see us, I glanced again at Chuck and then at our son. When I learned that night more than three years ago that God had a plan for me as a mom, little did I know that His plan was going to take me on an incredible journey of life and self-discovery. At the moment, my faith in His goodness comforted me and gave me strength to face whatever Dr. Salman would tell us.

3

The Diagnosis

Miss Debbie was the nurse assigned to Ben's case. She walked slowly into the waiting room and looked right at me. Chuck and I immediately stood as if she were a surgeon coming out of an operating room with the report of our loved one's condition.

"Hi," she said, "are you Benjamin Klassen's mom?"

I nodded and studied her. She had a concerned but friendly expression on her face and a very soft look in her eyes. Under the stress of the circumstances I should not have been interested in the least in her footwear, but when she first stepped into the waiting room, before noticing anything else, I immediately recognized her running shoes. The shoe style was the same that I had chosen for myself, and they were white and blue. Unlike mine, hers were very clean. She was dressed in white denim pants and wore a white, long-sleeved turtleneck shirt beneath her short-sleeved, blue staff polo. She was holding a ballpoint pen and what looked to be the few papers I had just filled out.

Without thinking I said, "I have those same running shoes." Hearing myself say the words, I realized how dumb and inappropriate they must have sounded.

Without hesitation, she replied, "Oh really? That's nice." She must have been thinking, "So what, lady? What does that have to do with anything right now?" but she said nothing. She switched the pen to her left hand, holding the papers and the pen together, and extended her free right hand to introduce herself.

After greeting her, Chuck stepped a few feet to his left to open the door of the small playroom and got Ben's attention while I introduced myself to the nurse. I did not initiate any further conversation; I was simply too nervous for small talk and was already embarrassed over what I might say.

A Test of Faith

The four of us went through a doorway and around a corner into a medium-sized exam room. The medical office was set up to welcome children and to ease their tensions, but I was finding that the atmosphere was relaxing me a bit, too. The exam room was painted a bright blue, and for only a moment, it reminded me of the morning sky that had started this already long day. This shade of blue, however, did not elicit a feeling of tranquility as the morning sky had. Instead, it was just a bold primary color painted on some walls. A Winnie the Pooh bubble machine sat on the counter next to the small hand sink, and beside that was a jar of the pointy plastic tips that the doctor uses on the end of the lighted otoscope when he looks into your ears. There was also a cart full of toys to the left of two chairs, and, across the room, a small stool on wheels, which was obviously for use by the head guy, the doctor.

"Please have a seat and get comfortable," Debbie said. "Dr. Salman will be right in."

We did sit, but not comfortably. I sat on the edge of my seat and held Ben on my lap. Chuck was a bit more casual as he sat with one leg across the other, tailor style, with his posture slightly relaxed. As soon as we were seated, not one minute passed before Dr. Salman joined Miss Debbie, Chuck, Ben and me. I was so incredibly thankful for his promptness. My nerves were frayed and the lump in my throat was growing so large that I was finding it hard to swallow. My mouth was dry and my eyes were burning although I had not yet shed one tear.

"Hello. You must be Mr. and Mrs. Klassen," Dr. Salman said in a thick Lebanese accent that I had trouble understanding. He offered a firm handshake first to me and then to Chuck. He then looked at Ben. Before he spoke, he squatted down to be eye level with the small child. In a kind and gentle manner, he offered his hand to Ben and said, "And you, young man, must be Benjamin."

Ben smiled as he nodded in affirmation.

Dr. Salman was very casual and relaxed like the rest of the staff seemed to be. I instantly liked him. He wore a polo shirt identical to his nurse's, with an embroidered logo of his name and that of the clinic on the left chest. The shirt was very wrinkled and looked as if he had slept in it, and I guessed later that he probably had. The man is more than dedicated to the children in his care, and I am sure now that by the time he saw Ben that Friday at 1:00 p.m., he had already put in a full day's work seeing all of the other sick children, inpatient and outpatient. He spoke slowly as he asked questions about our medical history as a family and about Ben's in particular.

"So, what concerns you today?" he asked.

We gave him all of the details we could think of about the bruises, the feet pain, the stomachache, and Ben's one complaint of a headache. We told him about every concern that we had had over the past few days that had brought us to this day of doctor visits. Chuck and I were in harmony as our words flowed perfectly with each other's help. When I would lose a thought, Chuck was able to finish the sentence for me. He knew just what I was trying to say as I was still trying to formulate the sequence of words and sentences in my head. The same was true for me when he lost track of his thoughts. Dr. Salman and Debbie concentrated on every word we said. By the time we finished in the blue room, Dr. Salman had completed a very comprehensive examination of Benjamin's body. He then left us to Miss Debbie for some other clinical tasks, specifically more blood work.

Ben was frightened now because he had just gone through the blood collecting process about two hours earlier and was well aware of the pain that the prick caused when it tapped into his finger pad. You'd think that with all of the medical technology in the world today that there would be a way to control the apprehension and pain that comes with what seems to be a simple test. Ben cried and wiggled around in my lap when he realized that he was going to undergo the procedure once more.

"No! I don't want to do this!" he exclaimed as he fought to pull his small hand out of Miss Debbie's.

I wasn't sure exactly how to calm him, yet I did not want to force him to be still. I knew he had to have this finger stick, so I whispered in his ear, "It'll go fast, Ben. You can do it."

We eventually made it through. However, the next step of drawing some tubes of blood from his small arm was unbearable. By this time we were all sweating, breathing heavily, and ready for a break.

"I'm so sorry, Ben, but I have to do this, honey," said Debbie. "Hang in there. You are being so brave."

Ben just looked up at her through his wet eyes.

Miss Debbie worked as quickly as possible and then followed her phlebotomy procedures with a genuine smile and another apology to Ben, with what I am sure was a little tear in her eye. She opened a small drawer to find a purple Band-Aid decorated with Casper the Friendly Ghost. "Look what I have for you," she said with great excitement as if she had some really special gift for our boy. She gently placed the Band-Aid into the break of skin opposite Ben's elbow. He was settling down and so were we.

Dr. Salman returned just a few minutes later and explained that he was very pleased and somewhat relieved by his initial exam of Benjamin. Ben's abdomen was soft, as it should be, and there was no evidence of swollen lymph nodes. His heart, lungs, thyroid, and joints all presented without any indication of a major problem. Besides being extraordinarily pale and having a few bruises on his shins, elbows, and back, he looked like a perfectly healthy boy. Even the doctor shared a glimpse of hope that just possibly, maybe, this was an iron deficiency, and all we needed were some serious vitamins in addition to more green vegetables, such as broccoli and spinach, in our diet.

We were led back to the fish tank waiting area once again and were asked to wait until the blood results came back from the lab. The blood was sent to the lab "stat," which meant that we were to know very soon if the centrifuge at the pediatrician's office was in fact malfunctioning. "Stat" also meant that in no time at all we would be done with visits to the doctor, we could stop by Walgreen's Pharmacy to buy some Fred Flintstone vitamins, and then we could go to the hockey game.

We waited and waited. I sat on a pale green chair with Ben on my lap. Chuck was tense as he sat to my right in the same type of green chair. It seemed like an eternity, but in reality the lab results came back in about thirty minutes. We were handed a report with the details of a complete blood count, but neither Chuck nor I had any true understanding as to what it all meant. The report was a standard piece of paper with a heading of "Outpatient Priority Results". Underneath the heading was a list of "Observations," which was simply a column of letter groups: WBC, RBC, Hemoglobin, Hematocrit, MCV, MCH, MCHC, RDW, PLT, AND MPV. Especially to Chuck, the letter combinations were like a foreign language. I recognized only a few of the abbreviations. The bottom half of the page continued with a list of twelve more letter groupings. To the far right, the paper had the word "Value" and then the words "Normal Range" typed. Printed in parentheses were the lower and upper limits, normal ranges, for each category.

Chuck wondered why these limits were printed on the page when the doctors knew from medical school what normal levels on blood studies should be. I thought having the ranges printed clearly on the report was really a good idea for both the doctor and the patient. It helped everyone to understand the laboratory's findings. Albert Einstein did not bother to remember his own phone number because he could always look it up on his Rolodex; so, in essence, it was the same for the doctor. He, of course, would know the relative norms for each blood test but need not be forced into remembering all of the specific ranges.

The final column of Ben's blood report was headed with the letters ABN for "abnormal." The notations there were the ones that really caught my eye. Below the ABN column were a series of "L's," and I noticed that absolutely everything on the list was abnormally low. Beads of sweat formed on my forehead. Something was very wrong with Ben's little body!

Soon after the results came back, we were moved from the main waiting area to wait in a private room until Dr. Salman and Miss Debbie were ready to meet again with us. I guess you could call this new room a combination of library, conference room, and project area. Although it was crowded with toys, a computer desk, and a disorganized pile of coloring books and markers, there was also an organized arrangement of scholarly journals on a shelving unit. I perused the binders of the stacks of periodicals and first noticed several black covers titled "Blood." I thought this was an odd and ominous color selection for the cover of a medical journal, so I paid little attention to it and continued my scan of the others in the neat row. The next set of journals was positioned vertically against the previous horizontal stack. This second section of thick magazines lifted my spirits just a tad when I saw that they were bright white with light blue printing. My interest was peaked momentarily as I read the title, *The Journal of Medical and Pediatric Oncology*. As I read these words, I somehow realized the immediate weight of the subject matter at hand and the possibilities of what might be wrong with Ben. I felt a little queasy, so I turned my back to the journals and held Ben tightly in my arms.

Dr. Salman and Miss Debbie entered the room together. The doctor sat down across from me, and Miss Debbie stood in the corner after she had closed the door. Their expressions revealed nothing.

The short moment of silence was deafening. I wanted to scream, "WHAT? WHAT IS IT?" I felt as if I could no longer breathe.

In his calming, baritone voice, Dr. Salman began his report while his nurse stood quietly. "I have some bad news for you. I believe your son has leukemia. According to his blood work, he is a very sick little boy right now, so I would like for you to have him admitted to the hospital so that we can do a bone marrow biopsy and then begin chemotherapy immediately."

Chuck gasped and turned to look at me. I felt like crying, but I couldn't seem to produce any tears. I held my son really close.

"Hey, Mommy, you're hugging me too tight!" Ben shouted.

I released my wrap around his little body, but I had to concentrate on the effort. In no other time in my life or his did I have such a desperate need to embrace him and protect him. I thought that if I held him closer, the words of the doctor would not touch him and therefore would not be true.

Chuck was the brave one. As he wiped the tears seeping from the corners of his eyes, he began to ask several questions. The conversation between the doctor and Chuck soon became jumbled in my brain. I was trying so hard to focus but could not absorb or process more than one or two words at a time. I thought to ask some questions, but I could not decide what I really wanted to say. Instead, I just sat quietly and listened. It was then that my eyes started to sting, and I had to bend my head down so that I could use Ben's shoulder to wipe my first tear.

I took a long, deep breath and concentrated on listening to Doctor Salman. I was thinking over and over again how wrong he had to be, so I am not sure of exactly how much of his explanation I really heard, if any. After all, he had just told us a couple of hours earlier that we were probably dealing with a vitamin deficiency or vitamin absorption problem, or maybe severe anemia. He had never mentioned cancer. It didn't seem possible that this could be happening, but it was.

I heard Chuck's next question loud and clear: "Doctor, if we choose not to do anything right now and we choose to go for a second opinion, what effect will this have on my son?"

The slightly overweight physician looked squarely in Chuck's eyes. "Sir, I can appreciate that you want a second opinion, and that is fine with me, but if you do not get this boy into a treatment protocol immediately, he will be dead in one to two months."

In the doctor's heavy words I heard the reality of what was happening. By 3:00 p.m. on that Friday afternoon, my excitement about the end of another successful workweek and the pending opportunity of a great weekend had evaporated. I felt as if a rug had been pulled from beneath my feet, knocking the breath from my chest and leaving me in a state of shock. I had just been told that my three-year-old son had cancer. I could hardly move as the words rang over and over again in my ears.

My son had cancer.

4

What Now?

I cannot remember much of the trip home from the hospital after that news. All I knew was that we had two hours to drive home, pack, find someone to watch Dana, and then return to the hospital to be admitted. Actually, I was still not convinced that we were going back to that hospital. Ever.

I called my dad from the cell phone in the car to tell him of the horrible news we had just received.

"Hi, Dad, it's me," I said.

He could tell immediately that something wasn't right. "Hi, Hun. What's wrong?"

I was still very stunned by the events of the day, so I was not interrupted by an emotional breakdown and was able to speak clearly but somberly to him. "Dad, I took Ben to the doctor this morning and something was wrong with his blood counts, so the doctor had us go straight to another guy in Ft. Myers. He says Ben has cancer."

"WHAT?" Dad said. It was more an exclamation than a question. "Tell me everything."

He was able to hear every word I said, but like Chuck and me, he was too shocked to comprehend or understand even one word of the conversation. Before I could complete my story, he interrupted with another question. "Where are you now?" I told him we were heading home and would be there soon. He promised that he would meet us at our house immediately so that we could go over the day's events again in person.

Miss Patty was still at our house finishing her day's work while Dana played quietly on the floor beside her. She and Dad had a chance to talk before we arrived, so she was up to speed on the news. When we finally walked in the door, Ben ran to her and wrapped his arms around both of her legs. She immediately picked him up, hugged and kissed him, and held him tight. I scooped up Dana and hugged her with all of my might. I looked at my sweet baby girl and wondered if her little body was as healthy and perfect as it seemed. My mind was going in a zillion directions.

My dad is a meticulous man and appears very calm. I have an incredible love and admiration for him, and I consider him my mentor, confidant, motivator, and, besides Chuck, my best friend. Actually, Chuck has told me many times that he has developed a deep bond with my father and considers him a best friend as well. For years I have admired my Dad's drive and the passion he has to learn; he inspires me to experience life and all that it has to offer. He is a man of great wisdom and strength, but he also has the heart of the kindest soul. He is professional, determined, and very sensible, yet he really knows how to have a good time, too. I even admire his stubbornness and tenacity because it completes him. He is a very critical thinker, which has brought him great success as a civil engineer, but he also sometimes thinks with his heart, which I suppose comes from being Italian. He is a lover. When times are turbulent, he is extremely analytical and always in control. He can stay grounded in the biggest of storms, and here we were right in the middle of a Category 10 hurricane, if there ever was such a thing.

My dad was our comfort and director on this day and for many days to come, and Chuck and I will be forever grateful. He started with, "Ok, let's relax a minute and think."

We sat in our family room and discussed the sequence of events step by step. We told him exactly what we could remember from our meeting with Dr. Salman. We told him that we had two hours before we had to be back at the hospital to be admitted. Things were happening so fast, and neither Chuck nor I could keep our composure any longer. We couldn't make decisions; we couldn't figure out what to do. We didn't know if we should take Ben back to the hospital or if we should make phone calls to arrange for a second opinion. We needed someone to tell us exactly what to do. We needed someone to tell us where to go and when to go. We needed someone we could trust to think clearly and rationally for us, yet at the same time, we needed someone who would think the same way we would under normal circumstances. We needed to be taken by the hand and then led along the right path because we simply were in no mental condition to make these critical decisions for Ben on our own.

A Test of Faith

Dad turned out to be that perfect thinker for us. Together we talked about flying to the best hospitals in the world—the University of Chicago, Loyola, St. Jude's, Sloan-Kettering, Duke, or even the Anderson Clinic in Houston, Texas—for an immediate second opinion. We talked about waiting until after the weekend and then contacting The Children's Hospital of Los Angeles, California. We then discussed the unknown capabilities of the small, local facility we had just visited.

We finally decided and agreed that we should call Dr. Salman back at his office and ask him if he was sure about everything. Did we really need to go back to the hospital that very night, or could we just wait until morning so that we could have some time to process everything?

I made the phone call. I volunteered to call because I wanted to ask Dr. Salman if he wanted to reconsider what he had said. I was hoping more than anything that maybe after he had had some time to think it over, he had decided he was wrong after all. Maybe he had decided that everything was ok and this diagnosis was not as critical as it sounded. Maybe he could at least give us the weekend to prepare ourselves to handle this situation.

It seemed as if the doctor was anticipating my call because I was not on hold long enough to plan my words before Dr. Salman picked up.

"Hello, Mrs. Klassen. Are you okay?"

His voice was full of compassion as he explained how he understood how hard this was for us. He talked to me like a close family member and said that Ben really needed to be in the hospital. His blood status was very dangerous, and there was definitely an element of urgency here. In addition, he already had called the blood bank and had several units ordered for cross typing and matching so that Ben could get some blood as soon as he arrived. The operating room was reserved for 6:00 a.m. the next morning, and the anesthesiologist had agreed to come in that early on a Saturday to help Benjamin undergo a bone marrow biopsy. He admitted that he could not be one hundred percent certain that we were dealing with leukemia, but he was confident that something very serious was wrong. He said the cells from the scheduled biopsy would give him the last bit of information he needed before ordering the chemotherapy drugs.

"No matter where you go in the entire world," Dr. Salman said, "the first step is going to be the same: a bone marrow biopsy to determine an exact diagnosis. Until we know exactly what is wrong, we don't know what treatment will be appropriate." He strongly encouraged me to bring Benjamin back to the hospital so that we could at least get this critical first step underway. We needed a confirmed diagnosis as soon as possible, but most importantly, we had to make sure that Ben was safe. The risks of having him at home, even for the night, were greater than the doctor wanted to take. Ben was in serious condition but could easily slip into critical condition if someone didn't help him immediately.

I thanked the doctor and hung up the phone. Chuck, Dad, Miss Patty, and I discussed every detail of the telephone conversation. Of course they already knew half of it from listening to the words that I had spoken, and they had already concurred that we would do as the doctor recommended. We all agreed that we needed to pack a few things and return to the hospital so that we could at least get started on the course of establishing a diagnosis. No matter where we decided to go for treatment, we first had to know what our problem was. No treatment anywhere in the world could be implemented until this first crucial step was completed.

I excused myself from the group still talking in the living room and headed to our bedroom at the far end of the house. My intentions were to go to the bathroom, brush my teeth, and wash my face. I thought this break would somehow refresh my soul and provide some much needed energy. I never made it to the bathroom, though, because I was immediately sidetracked when I entered our bedroom and saw the telephone at the corner of my nightstand.

I reached for the phone and dialed the home number of our friend and pastor. Rick answered on the second ring and listened quietly while I explained our circumstances. When I finally finished, Pastor Rick asked what he could do first to help and offered to meet us either at home or at the hospital. I decided that we were ok for the moment but asked him to pray with me. We prayed over the phone, and as I listened to his voice on the other end of the line, the tears fell like a waterfall from my eyes.

I learned later that after we talked, Pastor Rick immediately called the very dedicated prayer directors at our church. Before we were even settled into our hospital room that night, these two ladies had

A Test of Faith

literally hundreds of people praying for Benjamin and our family. A prayer chain began that night that was linked together by nothing but love, and in the tough months to come, it was never to be broken.

5

The Drive Back

Benjamin had always been a very smart little boy. I should have known that he had been listening to every word that was spoken throughout this day that was forever changing our lives. It was not until we were on our way back to the hospital around 5:00 p.m. that he asked, "Mommy, what is 'likema'?"

Neither Chuck nor I could figure out what this sweet boy, so safely buckled into his car seat, was asking. It took us four tries before we finally figured out that his question was "What is leukemia?" I was shocked when I realized what he was asking. As I turned as far around as I could from within my front passenger seat shoulder strap to somehow answer his question, I struggled to plan an answer in my head. I looked at Chuck, who had both hands gripped tightly on the steering wheel. His knuckles were white but not as white as his face. I thought I could see his pulse pounding in his neck. I glanced back at Ben, who was patiently waiting for my answer. I surprised him by unbuckling my seat beat and crawling across the center console into the back seat beside him.

Ben laughed. "Mommy, what are you doing, you silly?"

I laughed, too, as I nearly did a flip trying to position my now contorted body beside him. Finally, I was right where I wanted to be.

I looked into Ben's beautiful green eyes and smiled widely at him. I was considering bringing up another subject to avoid his question. I wanted to ask how his morning at preschool had been and what song he sang in front of the class. Since he was born, he had been naturally social with the personality of a true extrovert. He was always bubbly, always smiling, always positive, and always having fun, and I was proud of his personality. Jesus was also very light-hearted, so to the best of my ability, that's how I wanted to teach my children to be.

Ben loved preschool just as passionately as I loved my life, and he looked forward to going three mornings per week. All of the children

A Test of Faith

were given the opportunity to sing before the class right after they all said the Pledge of Allegiance. The teacher said that this was a confidence builder in the young ones, and I completely agreed. We loved to rehearse at home for his big rendition before his new friends.

I never did ask this question about school because as soon as my seat belt clicked, Ben repeated his question. "So, Mommy, what is 'likema'?"

Three years old, yet so intelligent and mature! I needed to tell him the truth.

When my mom was sick with cancer, I was very sensitive to what others would say to her or around her. It upset me when people whispered condolences as if she weren't sitting right there. At the end, people acted as if everything was perfectly fine, and they would even go to the ridiculous extremes of lying to her about what the doctors were saying or her true chances of survival.

Mom was an incredibly smart and sensible woman. She was nearly six feet tall and gorgeous. Near the end of her life, her 150 pounds had melted to maybe 110, and her skin was so jaundiced that it was more of a deep yellow or rich bronze in color rather than its usual healthy appearance. Her skin color resembled a deep orange sky right after sunset, and I thought she was still the most beautiful woman I had ever seen.

In my eyes, she was the best grandmother in the world, and she adored Ben. I knew she was very sick, and I knew deep down that only a miracle from the heavens could save her from the wild beast of cancer loose in her body. I also knew that she would never see Benjamin grow into a man, and she would never meet Dana. Everyone knew the reality of the situation no matter how hard it was to accept. I believe, however, that she wanted to be told the truth because she already knew the truth. I will be forever thankful that I sat at her side one day and spoke from my heart. We talked about Jesus and his promise of salvation through Grace alone and about Heaven. We spoke about miracles and the probability that one was not going to happen with her cancer. I answered her "why?" questions the very best I could. The most important thing I could do for her was to be there and tell her the truth about Jesus, as I knew it, and promise to her that I would be the best mom I could be to my children. With her incredibly weak and feeble body, she hugged me and said thank you. I work every day with Ben and Dana to keep that promise.

I was not about to share with Ben my thoughts and feelings about his condition or the technicalities of cancer, but I felt I certainly could not leave his question unanswered. I was not going to lie to him. He was smart, and the months to come were not going to bring just everyday trials. He certainly needed to know something, so I began.

I started with a desperate and most sincere prayer to God in Heaven. I begged from my heart and spoke from my deepest soul to the Creator I had come to know over my thirty-four years. I sat beside my son and gave thanks to God for all he did for me with His Son, and I asked for help. I pleaded for help. I told Him how much I could not do this on my own and asked, "Dear Father, PLEASE HELP ME. PLEASE!"

From that moment on, I swear I did not feel alone. Something was happening that would change me forever.

I started to tell my boy about "good guy" cells and "bad guy" cells. I tried my best to explain. "Ben, none of us did anything wrong, but somehow, bad guy cells got into your little body."

Ben said nothing. He just looked intently at me and listened, so I continued.

"Dr. Salman is going to help us get rid of those bad guy cells, ok?"

Ben nodded.

"We're going to listen to everything Dr. Salman tells us to do, and we are going to do it. Mommy and Daddy are going to be close by you every minute, and you will be just fine, champ. We have some fighting to do, but we're strong and tough, right?"

I told him about how the good guy cells were going to have to beat up those bad guy cells and get them out of his little body forever. I told him we were going to go to the hospital, and we were going to sleep there for a few days so that we could make the good guy cells strong and the bad guy cells gone. I told him everything I so desperately wanted to happen right now.

He looked at me with a very serious expression. He sat quietly for a moment as if he were concentrating deeply on all that I had said. It was almost as if he were trying to process the words and the weight of the subject. It was as if he were convincing himself that I was right, that we did have work ahead, and that we could do it. When he finally spoke, he asked, "Who's going to watch my little sister, Dana?"

My heart melted before he even finished. Here we were about to embark on the journey of saving his life, and his biggest concern in the entire world was his little sister.

I messed up his beautiful blond hair and gave him a huge kiss on the cheek.

"Don't worry, honey. Miss Patty and Grandma will watch Baby Dana for you."

6

Admitted

That first night in the hospital came and went without a minute of sleep. The activity in room 2806 was like a busy subway turnstile. As one nurse would leave after checking Ben with the thermometer and blood pressure cuff, another would enter with bags of fluid to hang on the IV pole beside him. Dr. Salman was directing staff, talking to us and to Ben, and making phone calls. The activity was exhausting for all of us but mostly for Chuck and me.

At around midnight Ben decided to sleep. I was relieved to see him resting after such a traumatic day of pokes and prods. I just wanted everyone to leave him alone for a few minutes. I was mostly relieved because I figured that if he was able to go to sleep, he was definitely feeling safe and secure with his parents at his side. Knowing that he felt secure with Chuck and me there gave me a comforting feeling; we had done something right as parents thus far.

As I watched him sleep, I realized that my job had only just begun. I was now a caregiver for someone with cancer. More specifically, I was a caregiver for a child with cancer. It was up to me to protect him and to make sure that everything that went on from this point forward was going to help him. I was going to be his liaison and his advocate. I was going to be responsible for all of the decisions to be made on his behalf, and I was going to be responsible for keeping a positive, healthy attitude through all of this. I had the biggest, most important job of my life thrown at me that day.

The procedure of the bone marrow biopsy went very smoothly the next morning. As promised, the only time that one of us was not at Ben's side was when we were not able to continue down the hallway leading to the operating room. As the gurney moved down the hall away from us, one of the O.R. nurses held Ben's hand and tried to comfort him as he watched us shrink into the distance. He cried a little but stayed amazingly strong. When he raised his little hand and gave us a cautious wave, I turned to Chuck, buried my head into his chest, and started sobbing. He held me tightly and cried openly, too. This was the first time we had cried together since we were given this shocking and awful news, and it was also the only time we were really alone to do so. The procedure downstairs took only about fifteen minutes, and we cried the entire time.

While Ben was in the operating room, Dr. Salman and the pediatric surgeon placed a small port-a-catheter under the skin in Ben's upper left chest. This device would be used for the administration of all medications, fluids, and chemotherapy. The invention of the nickel-sized device was nothing but genius. To not have to poke the patient for every procedure during cancer treatment, which literally meant hundreds and hundreds of times, was lifesaving in itself.

During the day, both Chuck and I had a chance to talk with some of the other parents, the nursing staff, and our families. We spent some time on the phone telling the horrible news to loved ones, and we spent some time reading. We had been given some literature early in the day about leukemia and learned that there were three different types. If we had to hope for one, our hopes were for Acute Lymphocytic Leukemia, ALL, because that type seemed to be successfully managed and easier to cure than the other types. So much research had been done on ALL that the success rate for cure was very good and improving every day.

Our fears lifted and our confidence grew as the hours passed. Saturday was a very long day for all of us and especially stressful for Ben, but by late afternoon he was resting well. Just before sunset I sat slouched in the hospital room's large pink recliner with a white hospital blanket wrapped around me. My stocking feet were propped up on my son's bed. The three of us were watching a Barney video that we had borrowed from the nurse's station. Barney and Baby Bop, the two colorful dinosaurs, were talking about Baby Bop's visit to the doctor. Ben watched and listened carefully as the two characters discussed the stethoscope and physical examination. I was comforted as I watched Ben respond to the story. I watched and smiled as my son took deep breaths just as the purple dinosaur did on the television.

I knew nothing about these kids' shows three years ago, but now I could tell you quite a bit about them. Some were pretty good in their teachings of manners, feelings, and friendships. Ben and Dana were allowed to watch two shows or two videos a day, so they did not have all that much TV in their daily routine, but the shows they did watch were positive, I thought. Barney was a favorite of Ben's, and under the circumstances, he was watching all of the TV he wanted. This was the fourth video of the afternoon.

I sat relaxing for the first time in over thirty hours. I scanned the room and saw the corner tabletop had already begun to fill with snacks, toys, and a couple of pieces of fruit from the breakfast tray. Extra straws from the other meal trays were still wrapped in their papers and waiting to be poked into plastic cups of apple or grape juice. Books brought in by a volunteer and a gift box from another one of Dr. Salman's young families occupied the rest of what had started as empty pink space. Oh yes, there was also a basket of "get well cookies" that my friend had sent. The cookies were shaped like Disney characters, and Ben had already bitten off Mickey's left ear. The water bottles beside this cookie basket were half empty, or you could say that they were half full. I had to remember that success in this experience was going to be all about attitude. I was peaceful. I was going to be ok with this. We could beat leukemia!

When the doctor walked in, I was not at all ready for the bomb he was about to drop.

"Hello, Benjamin. Hello, Mr. and Mrs. Klassen." Dr. Salman sat on the straight-back chair provided for visitors. With little facial expression, he continued. "I am afraid I have some unsettling news. The pathology report from the bone marrow biopsy this morning has come back, and the cells do not resemble those of a leukemia."

My first reaction was to jump and shout, "YES! Thank you, Jesus!!!" but something in the doctor's manner made me hesitate. I watched him as he stared at the floor for what seemed like an eternity.

When he finally looked up, he said, "I believe your son has a very rare form of childhood cancer called neuroblastoma." He did not say another word for several seconds. He was very somber and very different from our first encounter in his office just one day earlier. For a moment it seemed as if he were trying to decide on the best words to use but could not come up with any to describe in real terms what this meant to us.

Chuck broke the silence. "What is neuroblastoma? Is it a type of leukemia?"

The doctor's expression grew even more somber. "Well, it is not leukemia; in fact, we wish it was leukemia."

The words rang over and over in my head. I looked at Ben, who was propped up into a semi-sitting position in his bed. His blond hair was messy and a little matted. He looked very pale and was beginning to show dark rings around his eyes. It amazed me that I had not noticed the black smudges under his eyes earlier. After all, they were very obvious and seemed to be growing worse by the minute. It was beginning to look as if he had smeared the black putty football players used to reflect sunlight beneath his eyes. And why was his skin looking more gray than pale now? I grew intensely nervous as I tried to listen closely to what the doctor had to say.

"Neuroblastoma is a solid tumor cancer that is very serious," the doctor continued. "It is a cancer derived from the nervous system. We do not know exactly how or why it develops, but it seems to have a congenital origin. This may have been growing inside Ben for a long time, or it could have started only weeks ago. It is too hard to say, but we do know emphatically that this is an extremely aggressive type of cancer, and we must find the location of the tumor immediately. I have ordered a CT scan that will take place in just a few minutes here and then a series of other tests that I will discuss with you in the morning."

Because he had mentioned that the cancer derived from the nervous system, I imagined a tumor that was comprised of a ball of nerves with an appearance very similar to what you would see if you removed the wrapping from a golf ball. I had this picture in my mind when I heard Dr. Salman ask, "Do you have any questions?"

"WHAT?" was my only response, but I didn't say it out loud. I had a zillion questions, probably more. I was so shocked that I didn't know where to start.

Chuck asked a few questions, but I can't tell you what they were or how the doctor responded. I remember only one question specifically. Chuck asked Dr. Salman what Ben's odds were. He wanted some statistics. Chuck wanted a number that could give us an idea of how bad things really were. Unlike Chuck, I did not want a number. I did not believe in "the odds."

"What are our chances?" he asked.

"All I can say, Mr. Klassen, is that you never know. You need to start living like a child and live for the moment."

I was thankful for the doctor's response. I learned later that Ben probably had less than a 30 percent chance of survival. I'm glad I did not know the odds back then. All I did know was that we were in some deep trouble, and I was scared like I have never been before.

The doctor was very patient with all of our questions. He answered as best he could and did not hesitate or show frustration when he was asked the same questions over and over again. He did not leave until he knew that we were at least ok.

It was about thirty minutes later when the orderlies came to the door with a stretcher to take us down to radiology. The doctor excused himself and said he would be available by phone all night and would see us in the morning. Ben's eyes were the size of silver dollars when he saw the cart roll up to his door, and he began to cry. It was obvious that he thought he was going to be taken away from us again, like when he had gone to the operating room earlier in the day. He started to whimper, so I sat beside him on the bed and put my arms around him. It took every bit of strength I had to hold back the tears. I had cried so much that morning that I really thought it was impossible to have more tears, but they were there and I had to fight them.

I was determined to not let Ben see me cry during this whole experience. I had a sense that if he saw me positive and relaxed during even the most trying of the times to come, that he would hold onto my strength and be ok. If he saw me cry, I knew he would be frightened. I wanted that less than anything in the world, besides this sickening diagnosis, of course. I don't know how it happened, but I composed myself almost instantly and did sort of a little cheer for my nervous son. "Cool Ben, let's go for a ride. This will be fun!" I said with enthusiasm.

I hugged him close and told him everything was just fine and that we were going to have some pictures taken.

One time, a long time ago, we had read a story together about Curious George, a monkey who went to the hospital because he had swallowed a puzzle piece. If you know the story, Curious George had to have an x-ray so that the doctor could see the piece in his tummy. The little monkey had to drink a white mixture, and then the man with the yellow hat stood beside him at the x-ray table, protected by wearing a lead apron, while the staff dressed George in a similar protective lead garment. The story had a terrific middle with some uneventful surgery and all of the usual trouble typical of Curious George adventures. About the time the man with the yellow hat and the little monkey were getting ready to drive home from the hospital, the doctor ran out to their car and gave them a small present. Curious George decided to wait to open it until he got home. To his surprise and great satisfaction, the little gift was the puzzle piece. At the end, the monkey and the man were very happy.

This story came to mind when I was hugging my son and calming him. "Ben, remember when Curious George went to the hospital?" I asked with great anticipation, knowing Ben would relate immediately. "Remember when he swallowed that puzzle piece and had to go to the hospital to take the x-ray?" I continued with excitement in my voice. "Well, guess what? We get to go take one of those x-rays right now!"

Ben looked at me bewildered at first, but then I saw the tension ease from his brow. "Will you wear the apron like the man with the yellow hat did, Mommy?" he asked.

Relieved, I said, "Oh yes, I sure will."

I prayed silently that the events to come would be easy for Ben. I prayed that I, too, could stay strong for him.

I climbed up onto the gurney first and then Ben sat on my lap. Chuck followed closely while pushing the IV pole and trying to keep all the lines and bags from tangling. A dark red bag of blood hung on the pole above Ben's head as it had for the past three hours. When the nurse had come in to hang the bag of blood, she told us all about the transfusion he was going to receive. The nurse stayed in our room for one hour to make sure that this very first blood transfusion went in safely and without incident. She was fantastic. All the women were. Dr. Salman's program was first class. He did not cut any corners and was very strict on how he wanted things done. We learned very quickly that his kids were number one, and he would give anything to make them better. His staff had the same attitude. They embraced us like family and did everything in their power from the second we entered the floor to make us feel the best we could ... all things considered.

Alison was beside us on the trip down to radiology. She was slowly pushing a drug called Versed into Ben's IV line to help him to relax when she asked, "Is your Mommy behaving up there, Ben?"

Ben giggled softly. The drug ordered to relax him so that he would hold perfectly still during the scan was starting to take effect.

His tiny little body, all thirty-five pounds, was beginning to grow more limp in my arms, and he was completely calm. I was very thankful that Alison came along with us because when we arrived at the CT room, we met the wicked witch of the West.

The radiology technician on duty that night had a very sharp and offensive attitude. She raised her voice when we were about twenty feet from the room. "Where is anesthesia?" she hollered down the hall.

Alison did not respond until we were close enough so that she would not have to yell to hold up her end of the conversation.

The woman howled again, "Where is anesthesia, I said?"

Alison looked at her and replied calmly, "None was ordered, but we're fine. This is a very good little boy. We shouldn't have any trouble with him, and besides, Mom is right here to help."

The technician yelled on and on about how she had never had a kid hold still for this test, and she was not going to waste her time this late at night doing a scan on a child who was not put to sleep. I started to get a lump in my throat and looked over to Alison for help. She was already turning bright red.

"You get your butt into that room and set up for this test right now, or I'm going to get Dr. Salman in here!" Alison said without a bit of hesitation. She barked orders to the CT technician and stressed that this was an emergency and that the order was stat, by the way, so the tech had better get a move on it. "NOW!" she yelled.

As I stood afraid to move a muscle, swallow, or blink, I found myself being really impressed with our nurse's boldness. It was then that I found myself trying not to smile. Alison was a toughie, and I was so thankful that she was on our side.

Ben was in a complete stupor from the drugs, so he wasn't concerned about anything in the entire world. He just rode on the gurney and accepted the transfer to the CT table with an intoxicated grin.

When we were all finished with the CT scans, we went back to Ben's room. Alison helped transfer his sleepy body to his bed, plugged in his pump, readjusted some of the pump's programs, and then organized some papers in her hand. The entire time, she spoke not one word. It was then that I noticed she was starting to cry.

"Are you ok?" I asked.

She turned toward Chuck and me. "I am so sorry for all that you had to go through down there," she said, "but I was so mad at that lady that I just had to take charge. She really was not going to do the scan."

I could tell by the cracking of her voice that she was desperately trying not to burst out into tears.

"I know I didn't act professionally," she continued, "and I am so sorry. It's just that I love these children up here so much that I cannot stand to see anything or anyone get in the way of their recovery. I love these kids." By this time, she really was crying. She was shaking and still very angry but trying so hard to be comforting to us.

"Alison, you were great down there," I told her. "Not to sound condescending or anything, but I was so proud of how you handled that lady and the entire situation. You were fantastic! Thank you," I said with heartfelt sincerity.

"Thanks," she said and smiled. I could tell that she was relieved that we were not mad at her. How could we be? She really did a great job for us and for Ben. We hugged, and I again felt reassured about all of Dr. Salman's staff. These nurses were there for their patients, and they were more than dedicated to their jobs.

All soon quieted down. When Ben was asleep and Chuck had dozed off, I went downstairs to the chapel. I knelt and folded my hands together close to my heart and prayed. I didn't think it possible, but I started to cry again. I didn't stop for a long, long time.

7

What Is It?

Dr. Salman was concerned about the well-being of not just his patients, but the families as well, so he had an education specialist on his team who worked closely with all of the families. Laura provided us with a wealth of knowledge on neuroblastoma. She was able to stand up to every challenge in our questioning. She was unbelievably helpful to us and ended up being our walking reference guide. I didn't need to search out the hospital's library or sit for hours figuring out this cancer, which would have required energy I did not have. She was a great asset to us, and she most certainly saved what bit of sanity we had left.

Because the information she provided was so detailed and extensive, she gave us a three-ring binder full of useful facts so that we did not have to try to remember all that she was saying. The front cover of the binder simply read, "Parent Manual: Pediatric Oncology Program." The eight tabbed sections were designed to be very helpful, but as I read through each section, I began to feel sick. The pit inside my stomach seemed to grow to the size of a bowling ball. The information was important, but the feelings it provoked were petrifying. I felt overwhelmed, kind of like when I was a new college student and the professor assigned what appeared to be all of the work required for the semester, when in fact it was the homework for one night. I felt as if there was no way that I could survive the experience.

I found time to study when I was at the hospital with Ben, and he was asleep. On my drives to and from the hospital, I read as much of an article as I could while waiting at stoplights. When I was home and Dana had gone to bed, I found it difficult to sleep, so I sat and read. Most of the time I sat at the kitchen table and read by the overhead light when the rest of the house was dark and quiet. Too quiet without Ben.

A Test of Faith

    I learned that every year in the United States alone, over 12,000 children are diagnosed with some type of cancer. Over 2,000 of these children die from this horrible disease, making cancer the number one killer of kids in this country. Kids are supposed to have little falls, bumps, bangs, and bruises, and maybe a few stitches now and then, but they certainly are not supposed to have cancer. It just does not seem fair. Adults often abuse their bodies with drugs, tobacco, alcohol, and lifestyle choices, so their environments can sometimes explain or rationalize an illness. Children, however, are so young that they have not had any chance to make decisions about the ill effects of some of these substances. They are just doing what is right. They are waking up in the morning excited to play and have fun, and they should have no other concerns. Especially not about how healthy they are. There is absolutely no rationalization for cancer in anyone, adult or child. Cancer is a violent and wicked illness, and it is an unfair deal of the cards. I wish it did not exist at all, but especially not in children.

    Included in the binder provided by Laura, tucked into the back pocket, was an excellent handbook written by Debra Wagner, MSN, RN, of the Association of Pediatric Oncology Nurses (APON). It was titled, "Neuroblastoma: A Handbook for Families." She wrote that neuroblastoma was a cancer that developed from nerve cells. There was no answer to explain the cause of this type of cancer. Surprisingly, sometimes infants were born with neuroblastoma, which suggested that it could occur while the unborn child's nervous system cells were growing and maturing in the womb. I read the section on the signs and symptoms of the disease and the usual location of the tumors. They could be found in many different parts of the body, but mostly they were found in the abdomen and on the adrenal gland, which sits on top of the kidney. Less frequently, neuroblastoma could be found in the head, chest, neck, or pelvis. I learned that this cancer was actually the third most common type of cancer in children, and its occurrence was very rare. Approximately 600 cases of neuroblastoma were diagnosed each year in the United States. Fifty percent of the children with this type of cancer were diagnosed when they were younger than two years of age. Overall, 75 percent of all children were younger than five years old when diagnosed.

    Defined in the handbook was the word *metastases* and also what it meant when the disease was *staged*. These were both terms that explained the location of the cancer and how advanced it was. To have metastases meant that the cancer had spread from the site of the original tumor to other places in the body. Usually neuroblastoma was called a silent tumor because in 70 percent of children with this cancer, the tumor had already spread before any signs of the beast were noticed or diagnosed.

The stages described were classified as I through IV, with I being the best. In stage I, the tumor was small and found only in the structure where it began. No spreading of the tumor had occurred. Stage IV was by far the worst. The tumor in this case had spread from its original location to a very distant area, such as bone marrow, liver, or lymph nodes. The way doctors attacked the cancer depended partially on the stage of the disease at the time of diagnosis.

The rest of the handbook told about the tests we should expect and what types of things we could do to get through all of this. I've learned that the Association of Pediatric Oncology Nurses (APON) is an excellent resource. The Association provides and promotes expertise in pediatric hematology and oncology nursing practice to its members and to the public. The patient education materials that the association offers are extremely helpful to anyone searching for information on this subject.

Nowhere in the handbook did it talk about prevention, and this was a question that worried me nearly every day and night. Although I realized that it was too late to do anything now, I needed to know if this cancer was somehow my fault. I wondered what I could have done differently to save Ben from all of this suffering. Was there any way I could have known about this sooner?

Other people began to ask me the same question, so I reached out for some answers. After some research, I have found that the answer to that question is yes. I was sickened when I learned that we could have prevented Ben from reaching a later stage of the disease by a simple urine test. If this urine test reveals elevated levels of catecholamines, or specific hormones better known as epinephrine and norepinephrine, this can be an indication that there is a problem somewhere in the body. These hormones have a tremendous effect on the nervous and cardiovascular systems, metabolic rate, body temperature, and specific muscle activity, so the body regulates them carefully via the adrenal glands. If there are too many catecholamines being synthesized in the body, they will be excreted through the urine, so a simple urine test can give the doctor very important information about the absence or presence of neuroblastoma. If certain levels are detected in infancy, the tumor can be located and then clipped out like a bothersome mole. Unfortunately, this urinalysis costs about $600, so insurance companies have opted not to make it a routine part of the infant's workup.

America is one of the only modernized countries that doesn't routinely check its newborns for the cancer. For example, Japan and all of the European countries have this urine test as protocol on a newborn. The philosophy in the United States is that if only a handful of children will be diagnosed with the cancer in a year, the probabilities are too low to make the test cost effective on everyone. I can completely understand this thinking from a financial perspective, but I think parents should at least have the opportunity to choose to have the test performed on a private pay contract. I understand that $600 is a lot of money for most people, but if I was given a thorough explanation of the possibilities and probabilities of neuroblastoma and was at least offered the choice to have the test performed on my children at my own expense, I think I could have made the decision and lived with the consequences. It would have been the same decision I had to make when I was pregnant and was offered genetic testing of the fetus that would indicate if my baby had Down's syndrome or other genetic abnormalities. I think I might have considered the offer to have the urine test done. If I were told that we could clip out a tumor and be done with it versus suffer the problems we had now with a fully metastasized, invading, life-threatening cancer, I think I would have had the test done. But who knows?

Neither Chuck nor I stopped our investigation of neuroblastoma with the materials provided by the staff at the hospital. We pored over most of my medical textbooks and searched the science of medicine for more precise information about the disease. The additional information I read was largely more technical but still helpful to me. I looked at work put out by *The New England Journal of Medicine*, *The Medical and Pediatric Oncology Journal*, and *The Journal of Clinical Oncology*. I was amazed and thankful for all the hard work and dedication of many scientists around the world. People were doing an incredible number of studies and experiments in laboratories for the benefit of others, and I soon realized just how important their efforts were to me as an individual. From then on, I saw that I was not the only caregiver for Ben in this picture. All of the physician-researchers working somewhere in labs studying cancer and neuroblastoma were also, although indirectly, caring for my son. It is because of these long hours researching in laboratories, in textbooks, and on computers that Ben had a chance to survive this cancer.

The literature on the particular cancer called neuroblastoma is depressing to read, to say the least. Every article, textbook, Internet piece, or other information that I could lay my hands on started with a sentence similar to this one: "Children with high-risk neuroblastoma have a poor outcome." Or, "The long-term survival rate for children with neuroblastoma is only 15 percent." Or, "Despite improvements in treatment and supportive care, most patients with high-risk neuroblastoma experience recurrence." After a while, I couldn't take any more. I wanted the facts, but only on my terms. I studied just what I needed to know about the basics of the disease so that I would be familiar with the terminology and the protocol. After that, I closed all the books and just concentrated on Ben. As far as he would ever know, the good guys cells were going to win. It was as simple as that.

I had to trust that God had a plan for this little boy. I knew that God did not mess around. When He has a plan, it is an awesome plan. I have snorkeled in the crisp, clear waters of the Florida Keys, stared into the midnight sky of Northern Michigan, hiked the Rocky Mountains, and witnessed the calving of a glacier at Glacier Bay National Park in Alaska. I have thought about the miracle of the sperm and the egg and then gazed with love at my perfect children at their births. I trust wholeheartedly that God has an incredible imagination, a wonderful sense of humor, and yes, always a perfect plan.

8

Taking Pictures

In the days that followed at the hospital, I was a wreck as I watched Ben become sicker and sicker. He slipped into a state the doctors referred to as DIC, or disseminated intravascular coagulation, which meant that a disease to the bleeding and clotting system in Ben's body had developed. He was not able to produce or maintain a healthy blood level on his own, and his body was no longer able to clot blood properly, so he was now technically in critical condition. If he were to start bleeding—for example, from his nose—chances were that they would not be able to stop it, and he would bleed to death.

As a result of Ben's DIC status, the mood in the room rapidly declined. We, including the doctor and nurses, were petrified with fear as to what could be next for Ben. The surgical site around the new port in his chest would not heal. Essentially, Ben's body did not have any capability to heal; it was struggling just to live. Because the incision site was still a mess, the nurses could not use the port as they had hoped, to administer medications, fluids, and the chemotherapy drugs that were going to be prepared in the pharmacy as soon as the doctor gave the order. Ben had to continue to have his left hand splinted on a piece of padded cardboard, and he could neither flex nor extend his wrist. The long, plastic IV tubing coming out of the vein on the top of his hand was taped for security in several places up his forearm. We were careful not to let anything get caught on that line. If the needle pulled out of his hand, the open wound would bleed. This would be an emergency. Furthermore, the nurses would have to start over in establishing an intravenous line, which meant another dangerous puncture wound to Ben's skin.

This restriction on the movement of his left hand made Ben even more uncomfortable and frustrated. He was growing more pale and much more irritable. I could see the agitation rising within him with every aspect of the hospital staff's care. He was becoming much less tolerant to anyone touching him or trying to help him. At times however, I could see a mood swing to extreme lethargy. Right before my eyes, he was doing exactly what the doctor had said he would do if we did nothing: he was dying. His little frame was growing thinner, and he wanted to sleep all the time. Every time he fell asleep, I wanted to run to him, shake his shoulders, and make him open his eyes. I wanted to say, "Please, please, open your eyes! Let's go play, let's read a book, anything, something! Please don't die, baby." I knew, though, that I had to let him rest.

It was eight days from diagnosis before we could start on a treatment program. We had to wait for the bone marrow cells to come back from a sophisticated lab in California called BIS. There they had a machine that would count out one million cells from the biopsy sample and then would study the DNA structure of each and every one. It was sensitive enough to find just one cell that was irregular, one malignant cell out of a million. The doctor was not going to begin pouring the gallons of poison called chemotherapy into Ben until he was absolutely, one hundred percent sure that we were dealing with neuroblastoma cells. I understood his reasoning and agreed, but at the same time, it was virtually impossible for me to watch, wait, and do nothing while my son lay in bed fading away from life.

While waiting for the results from BIS, we did not just sit idly. Christmas was coming, and I tried to get Ben excited about the holiday, but not even talk of Santa or presents or Baby Jesus in the manger cheered him up. Fortunately, Dana was too young to know much about Christmas, and regretfully, I let the special day slip past her.

We continued to gather bits of new information that provided the doctors with a greater understanding of the disease that had invaded Ben's young body. In order to collect this additional information, however, we had to subject Ben to more studies and tests. The new pieces of information about the disease gave us all a better insight as to what we were dealing with, but again, because we could not start on any treatment until the cell studies returned from BIS, the unfavorable results of each test just elicited more and more calamity in Chuck's heart and mine. I felt as if I were being buried in sand, an experience I had as a kid at the beach. With each new piece of information on Ben's failing health, I was finding it more and more difficult to move. The weight of the sand was growing heavier and heavier.

The results from the CT scan, or "red-light-green-light machine," as Ben eventually started calling it, came to us during this waiting period. The films taken during the night of the "brawl" with Alison and the CT technician showed a large tumor on the adrenal gland above Ben's left kidney. The tumor measured six centimeters by six centimeters, which was about the size of a tennis ball, but unfortunately, it was poorly defined. Dr. Salman came into our room to tell us that he thought that this tumor was, in fact, the source of the cancer.

"Look here," he said. The black and white film resembled a traditional x-ray but offered views of the tumor from every angle. He held it up to the window beside Ben's hospital bed and used his pen to outline the tumor. "As you can see, the tumor is sitting right on top of Ben's left kidney. This is where the adrenal gland is located."

Remarkably, I could see exactly what he was talking about. Chuck and I asked questions about the characteristics of the tumor, such as how thick was it, was it actually part of the kidney, and could they tell if it was alive and still growing. I also asked the doctor if he was sure that this was a neuroblastoma cancer because the tumor looked to me like it was actually part of the kidney. I wondered if it was possibly a Wilm's tumor or a mass other than neuroblastoma.

"Because of Ben's rapidly changing presentation and because of the cells that we studied from the biopsy, I am convinced that this is not a Wilm's tumor or malignancy of the kidney," the doctor answered. "I feel very strongly that Ben has neuroblastoma."

"Can't we operate now and remove the tumor?" I asked.

I suppose my question was what anyone would have asked. It just seemed sensible to remove the source of the cancer. Unfortunately, things were not that easy for a couple of reasons that Dr. Salman explained. First and foremost, Ben was too weak and too ill to be able to survive a major abdominal surgery. Second, the tumor looked as if it were wrapped around the abdominal aorta and had tentacles reaching out to other vital structures in the region. There was no way a surgeon could go in and remove this tumor that was so intertwined in vital organ tissue without killing Ben.

The CT scan also showed some shadows on Ben's head. It was too difficult to tell if the cancer was in the brain, just on the surface of the brain, or only in the skull, but generally, because the disease had spread so far from its original site, the outlook for Ben was grim. Before we could panic, however, we needed more information about the exact locations of the disease. It was not fair to jump to conclusions or formulate opinions or make important decisions about anything until we had gathered all the facts. As soon as we had a clear picture in our minds of what was happening, we could safely plot a course of action and prepare ourselves for anything. Making a move before we had that clear picture would most certainly have led us down a path of destruction. In particular, Dr. Salman needed more evidence and more information to prove that the cancer, without a doubt, was what he thought it was. Furthermore, he needed conclusive evidence and specific details of any locations where the disease had spread in Ben's body so that he would know exactly what to do to treat it and the best way to do so.

The next study that Dr. Salman ordered was an MRI. The magnetic resonance imaging machine, better known as the MRI, was located at the main hospital up the road, about seven-and-a-half miles north of where we had been admitted. The Healthpark Hospital, was part of the Lee Memorial Health System, but Healthpark was sort of a satellite or secondary facility located on its own campus. It was built only about fifteen years ago but had quickly become the site for several specialties of medicine, such as open heart surgeries, obstetrics, neonatal care, and, of course, thankfully, pediatrics at the part of the facility known as The Children's Hospital. Like all of the hospitals of Southwest Florida, it was often filled to capacity with inpatients occupying every bed, and it was already undergoing expansion. Although this hospital was well equipped with excellent diagnostic tools and machinery, it did not have the luxury of an on-site MRI. We needed an MRI scan of the head to see exactly what was going on in Ben's brain. Because Ben was so critically ill and because he still required constant fluids and medications intravenously to keep him as stable as they could, the medical staff decided that the only option we had was to transport him to the north facility for the MRI scan by ambulance.

"Guess what, Ben? We're going to go for a ride in an ambulance. What do you think about that?" Chuck asked him.

Ben's passion for sports was only slightly greater than his love for emergency rescue vehicles. His bedroom was full of fire trucks and ambulances, so he was pretty happy about going on this ambulance ride. He didn't have the energy to show any bubbling enthusiasm about the trip, but I could see the sparkle in his eyes when we told him of the plan.

He was quiet during the whole trip and remained still on the stretcher while Daddy held his hand. A nurse sat in the corner by the back doors. When we arrived at the main hospital building and pulled into the emergency room, Ben had just one question that he asked with a very weak and raspy voice:

"How come we didn't get to turn on the loud sirens and blow the air horn?"

The MRI was a very intimidating machine for even the bravest of boys, and Ben could not be expected to hold completely still by himself in that tunnel of jackhammers. The anesthesia used to sedate him was a thick, white concoction that closely resembled whole milk, and it knocked him out almost instantly. I stood in a room full of computer equipment and technical instruments and watched through the glass as my baby slowly became encased in this monstrous block of machine. I prayed that the spots they saw in his head on the CT scan were not actually in the brain. I knew of the blood brain barrier and understood that if the cancer had spread into that vital organ, we would have a tough time getting the chemotherapy to work. If that were the case, Ben probably could not survive this battle. I watched the computer screen as the image slowly produced Ben's brain, and I pictured the image to be perfect. I willed it to be. I prayed for it to be perfect.

****

The days prior to beginning treatment passed slowly. Chuck and I took turns staying with Ben every night at the hospital so that one of us would be home with Dana. We needed to hold her, love her, and be close to this precious time of her infancy. She was sensing that something unusual was going on in our home; it was quite evident to even a seven-month-old. I was so worried about her, too. I was afraid that if we did not put forth a valiant effort to keep her life as normal as possible, the separation and stress of the situation would scar her for life. Her joyful, loving, outgoing personality could easily turn to being withdrawn, insecure, and resentful. I could not let that happen.

Sandie Klassen

It was a long and agonizing time before we finally received the results from the BIS lab and a confirmed diagnosis. As we waited, Ben grew worse every day. His cheeks looked drawn, and the life in his eyes faded. He lost his desire to eat or play and became easily combative when we made any suggestion to coax him out of bed. He complained of needing to throw up, which I imagine was provoked by the severe pain in his feet and abdomen. He cried frequently and often for no apparent reason. The room would be quiet, no staff would be around, no one would be touching or talking to him, yet, he would burst out into tears. I felt more than helpless.

Many times throughout the days he would scream out for someone to rub his feet. "Help, ouch! My feet, my feet … Please make the pain stop!"

Either Chuck or I would rush to his side and begin rubbing his small feet and toes. Ben would calm down after a few minutes, but by the time he did, his forehead was usually wet with sweat.

Late in the evening on that eighth day, we finally began to battle the cancer with chemotherapy treatment. The chemotherapy and rigorous "first course" of treatment seemed endless. One, two, or sometimes several chemotherapy drugs were used over a short period of time, which we learned was called a "course." After the completion of a course of chemotherapy, the patient had to rest and allow the body to recover before another course could be administered.

Ben was able to do nothing because the cancer had seemingly taken over inside his little body. He had a difficult time standing and most certainly could not walk. His leg strength was all but depleted, and his motivation to work through the progressing weakness was lost. We were now on a racecourse; it was the treatment and our prayers versus the pathetic disease called neuroblastoma.

We celebrated Christmas at the hospital and did our best to make it special for the children. The hospital did, too. They allowed a husband and wife dressed as Santa and Mrs. Claus to come onto the floor and go into the children's rooms. This completely unselfish couple forfeited their own holiday at home with family to be with us strangers. The gifts they purchased were from their own hard earnings, and the love they shared was heaven sent. Pastor Rick came late in the evening and shared a Christmas message and bedside communion with us. We certainly did have a celebration on that Christmas—a celebration that continues every day.

A Test of Faith

We were lucky enough to be able to go home for a few days to start the New Year. Chuck and I never could have imagined that when we arrived for admission to the hospital that first Friday evening, it would take nineteen days to get Benjamin stable so that we could go home again. It just didn't seem possible that life could take such a sharp and sudden turn, but it had. I couldn't believe that I had awakened one morning feeling healthy, vigorous, and passionate about the new day and life and then was unable to return to my own bed for nearly three weeks, barely escaping death on the way.

Ben's official diagnosis was neuroblastoma, stage IV, with metastatic disease to the bone marrow, liver, lymph nodes, and extradural frontal and temporal bones. The cancer had not penetrated the protective covering of the brain, so we were fortunate that his brain was clean and healthy. Perfectly healthy. God was listening. I was convinced of this. I had to trust Him and keep my faith as strong as I could. I had to stay focused because the real fight was now going to begin.

9

The Protocol

It was now time to start the journey of killing the bad guy cells, and we were ready. With Ben's cancer, there were eight different drugs used in the chemotherapy. The names of the drugs were long and sounded very threatening: Carboplatin, Cisplatin, Cytoxan, Doxorubicin, Etoposide, Ifosfamide, Thiotepa, and Vincristine. They were all called "cancer-fighting medicines." All I could pray for was that each had its boxing gloves on and that it was ready for the biggest fight since its development. We were not going anywhere until the drugs successfully killed every cancer cell in Ben's body. Only the strong survive, and we were going to be the definition of strength.

We were told that these drugs, in the combination to be used in Ben's small body, were going to be equivalent to sixty times the chemotherapy dosage given to an adult. That is sixty times more poison than they would give a grown-up person. How could they do this? It will kill him, I thought.

Dr. Salman explained that a child's body grows so fast, and the cells reproduce and change so quickly, that it is more resilient than an adult's body. Theoretically, a child's body could recover from the intensity, volume, and potency of the drugs. The doctor's explanation sounded reasonable, so we hung on to our hope of success. We knew that if the drugs were not used, Ben would certainly die, so we wanted whatever the pharmacists and doctors could develop. Destroying this monster inside Ben was our total focus.

The doctor promised that Ben would be very, very sick over these next several months while undergoing chemotherapy, but we had no choice. We really didn't. There was nothing I wanted more in this entire world than to save my boy's life. I wanted his life back so badly that I would have traded my own for it. I saw so much hope in him, so much future. He was only three years old. He still had so much life ahead of him. There were still so many things for him to see, to learn,

A Test of Faith

and to experience. He needed to have the wonderful opportunity to stumble and fail and then to start over and feel the joy of success. We did not have a choice but to win this cancer battle.

The "protocol," or treatment plan, for this deadly cancer called neuroblastoma was very structured, and it looked to me to be very difficult. The protocol was to have six courses of chemotherapy at the most intensive level possible, but each course was to be separated by a two-week recovery period. The chemotherapy portion of the protocol would last for a total period of five or six months. After that, or during that time, as soon as possible, the solid tumor would be removed surgically. Next would come intensive radiation to all the sites that had shown evidence of disease. The protocol would culminate with a bone marrow transplant. If all went well, the treatment would be completed within twelve months of its commencement. The program designed to battle this devastating disease would inflict tremendous pain and suffering but could offer no guarantee of a cure. It was all up to Ben and God.

The science of chemistry is a fascinating field. To consider that there is an ability to study the composition, structure, properties, and reactions of matter at its most basic state—atomic and molecular levels—is almost too implausible to be believed. For me, advanced organic chemistry was the most challenging course required in college. The abstract concepts of the carbon-loaded hexagons were beyond my mental capabilities, so to this day I have the greatest regard for the biochemists, physicians, and pharmacists who work together to create the wonders of chemotherapy. The idea that one would even consider introducing such potentially lethal substances into the human body is astonishing to me, particularly after seeing the severe reactions to these compounds. There has to be an element of trust that these scientists know exactly what they are doing in designing these potent drug combinations. There has to be a trust that the drug can go from laboratory theory and experimentation, to real patient.

The chemotherapy to be used on Ben was essentially a blend of poisons that would target and kill the cancer cells that had made their way through his body. The chemotherapy was presented in liquid form to Ben, and the bag of potent chemicals was clear and unassuming in its appearance. The modesty of the bag was deceiving. The only clues to tell us that something different was going into

Benjamin's body were the protective clothing worn by the nurses and the big, red, "Danger" labels plastered all over the bag. The nurses had to be completely covered from head to toe before they could handle these drugs. They wore hats, goggles, masks, gowns, gloves, and foot covers.

The drugs were dangerous. They were designed to hunt down, attack, and destroy any fast-growing cell in the body, and cancer cells were extremely fast at reproducing and growing. Unfortunately, other normal, healthy cells in the body grow fast, too, and the drug was not entirely specific or selective to cancer. Other cells that could be attacked were cells of the mouth and digestive track, skin, all blood cells (including those that serve as the backbone of the immune system), liver and kidney cells, and reproductive cells (the sperm and the egg). Hair cells are also extremely fast growing, and that is why patients on extensive chemotherapy lose all or most of the hair all over their bodies.

People who are bald from chemotherapy are truly stunning and graceful in my eyes because I know exactly what they have gone through to lose their hair. A person's entire being changes when he or she is diagnosed with cancer, and there are so many physical and emotional obstacles to overcome during the course of recovery. The sight of oneself or one's child without any hair can, at first, be frightening and defeating.

When I first watched Ben's hair begin to fall out, I felt saddened and anxious about his new look. Stupidly, I was concerned about how others would look at him and treat him. I was worried that people would look at me with disgust assuming that I had done something wrong to cause my son to be punished by being diagnosed with cancer. Receiving a frightening medical diagnosis tears your mind apart. You no longer think rationally, and you mentally seem to blow everything out of proportion. I was initially unreasonable in my thinking about Ben's hair loss, but I quickly adjusted and came to my senses. I realized that no one was going to look at my son and then blame me.

God does not punish people for anything except neglecting the fact that Jesus is His son. Sometimes He allows things to take their course because He has a great purpose planned for the experience. After I realized this, I accepted Benjamin's baldness. It actually comforted me. I felt that it brought attention to him, and just possibly it was part of God's plan. People would look, they would wonder, and maybe they would see their own health and life in a different light.

I see baldness resulting from chemotherapy as powerful, brave, courageous, and beautiful. I see chemotherapy baldness as a message to others to take note of themselves and their purpose in life. Maybe this sounds too deep or philosophical, but it makes sense to me. These bald patients are strong and determined people, and I think they are remarkably inspiring. Especially the children.

****

Although we had completed one course of chemotherapy in Florida, we still were not sure at that point if we were in the right facility for treatment. We had a very difficult time when it came to making a decision of where to go for Ben's neuroblastoma treatment protocol. This decision was the first of many we were going to have to make for him, but it seemed the most critical. We would never forgive ourselves if we did not get the best care available for him, so we were ready to travel to the ends of the earth to arrange for him to see the best doctors and to be in the best hospital. We started asking some serious questions and had everyone we knew doing as much research as they possibly could. We learned of an organization called the Children's Oncology Group, or COG. We realized that we needed a medical team that was heavily involved with this organization, which was motivated more by the success of curing the patient than money. We searched for a treatment program that would care about us as people, not just as a disease.

We learned this: each cancer basically has its own recipe of chemotherapy, which is the combination of drugs designed to destroy the specific disease on hand. Pharmacists, physicians, and scientists have worked closely together to find the perfect mix of the appropriate ingredients and have found each special blend to be lethal to certain types of malignant cells. With adult cancer victims, each individual hospital or institution has an oncology team, which has its own preferred way of treating cancer patients. Each team relies heavily on its own doctor's research, the team members' treatment experiences, and the doctor's best judgment. In addition, of course, everyone reads everyone else's published literature and research outcomes in the field, attends conferences, and shares ideas that promote a cure for the patient afflicted with cancer. Nevertheless, there is a ton of competition between institutions, and it is probably rare for anyone to share every detail of promising lab results and potential successes, just in case they might result in a windfall. Such a discovery could certainly put an institution on the map, and such a windfall would, without a doubt, line someone's pockets nicely.

Sometimes it seems to me that successful cancer treatment is only about money. I wish that the drive for a cure was motivated by a desire to help mankind or to rid the world of pain and suffering, but deep down I think the focus is money. It is a matter of who can be the best, who can have the best outcomes, and who will develop the best reputation and, therefore, draw in the most patients. Whoever attracts the most patients will, of course, generate the most revenue, so there you have it: money. The drug companies would flock to that leading institution, researchers would share more secrets with the drug companies funding their studies, and the circle of financial hopes and dreams would grow thicker, deeper, and more entwined. Someone is going to make it big from this competitive attitude and drive, so there is a bit of secrecy and game playing. It's strictly my opinion, and I hope that I am totally wrong on this, but it just seems to be the case. Nearly every person you talk to on the street has had a broken heart and family because of cancer. This disease has devastated many people. All of us who have been affected don't care about money and profits; we want nothing more than to stop this evil menace called cancer.

The truth is this: ours is a society driven by politics and money, and however bold or controversial my opinion may be, I really think it is true that money is the primary driving force behind medicine's answer to cancer. Sometimes I wonder if a cure for cancer has already been determined, but no recognition is allowed because of the economic impact such a cure would have on the world. Just think of all the drug companies, hospitals, equipment manufacturers, laboratories, medical supply companies, doctors, nurses, and other businesses and people that could potentially be closed or put out of work if cancer were cured. Hmmm. Keeping a major discovery secret or holding back on finding a cure for cancer could just possibly be happening. Think about it.

With kids, however, everyone wants a cure. Everyone wants to obliterate cancer in children. It is too gut wrenching to see these young people, who are just getting started on the adventure and gift of life, taken down by such a horrible sickness. For this reason, most doctors cannot think of money when it comes to the little innocent children who are diagnosed each year. In these cases in particular, it is ethically and morally wrong to be motivated by anything but the will to preserve life itself. To do that, doctors have to want to find a cure for cancer.

Motivation by money may work some of the time, but money is of little relative value when it is your child who is in bed with this life-threatening illness. After all, what if you were told that your own son or daughter had cancer? If you were a doctor or hospital administrator who was told this news, you would be devastated. If your life had been based only on greed for money and fame, you may have been able to tolerate the diagnosis of cancer in your ninety-year-old grandmother, but if you were anywhere near human, you would be sick beyond reason to hear this news of your child. You could never forgive yourself for not allowing the research to take place or the sharing of information with your competitors.

So, curing children of cancer is not about money. Evidence of this is that doctors and research institutions involved with childhood cancer have joined forces. Every discovery, no matter how insignificant it may seem, is shared with all of the others so that every bit of energy and intelligence are working together to finish the puzzle; they are dedicated to finding the cure and conquering the disease. When the doctors, hospitals, and research institutions learned how valuable this sharing of information was, they founded what were once called the "POG" and "CCG." "POG" was the Pediatric Oncology Group, and "CCG" was the Children's Cancer Group. These two groups were still separate when we started this ordeal, and, believe it or not, even they have now merged. Today there is just one group with many members working together to beat pediatric cancer, and it is called the "COG," Children's Oncology Group.

This very prestigious international organization selected Dr. Salman and The Children's Hospital to be a part of the group in 1998. Now everyone dealing with cancer in kids can participate in the COG on one team, and this is a team that wants nothing more than victory! Isn't this the most exciting news that you have heard in a long, long time? Because of the efforts and compassion of this group of dedicated people, I truly believe that we will rid this world of childhood cancer soon. We have all the top medical scholars joining forces, working together, and pulling as a team, all for a common cause. We have the ivory tower of academia striving for a once-and-for-all cure to childhood cancer. NO MORE CANCER IN KIDS. Cancer is too lousy of a straw to draw, so let's get rid of it. COG is on the right track.

Because of the unselfishness of many loving hearts and brilliant medical minds, and because of the development of the COG, every pediatric cancer institute that wants to be a part of the COG and is accepted can share the same protocols for neuroblastoma. Therefore, no matter where we decided to have Ben treated, he would receive the same protocol for the disease. After learning this, it made sense for us to stay as close to home as possible for Ben's treatments. Staying close to home meant that we would be near the people who loved us and who could help us. Staying close to home meant that at least every other night we could be in our own bed, and we could somehow maintain a bit of normalcy for Dana. Also, we could keep up with our work at the clinic.

Because Chicago, Texas, New York, Tennessee, and even North Dakota were going to use the same cookbook for Ben's chemotherapy recipe, it only made sense to stay in Ft. Myers, Florida. To this day, I am so glad that we stayed. At The Children's Hospital, we were a family. Ben was a special little boy, and Dana was welcomed with open arms, too. We were everything in the hearts of those who cared for us, and I don't think we even had a number. It sure didn't seem like it, anyway. Ben was Ben, and we were his family. All of the kids, parents, and staff were family. We were fighting for each other, and we were doing everything we could to help each other get through this battle.

There were only six rooms on the children's oncology unit, so the nursing-to-patient ratio was exceptional. Dr. Salman was there day and night if someone needed him. He was fighting for us, too, but not just from a medical perspective. He wanted our hospital room to be a safe place and as happy as it could be under the circumstances.

One Saturday morning Dr. Salman came into the hospital with his two young children and surprised all of us with a huge pancake breakfast. He set up a long table by the conference room and supplied balloons, orange juice, milk, lots of whipped cream, and all of the toppings for pancakes that you could imagine.

A Test of Faith

When I told Ben about the surprise party, he looked at me with tired eyes and a soft voice and asked, "Really? Can we go?"

"Sure, let's go," I said. I was so relieved that Ben was willing to do anything! Although he was still very weak, his body and spirit were beginning to strengthen once again.

Chuck and I helped Ben out of bed, and he stood holding onto the bed while we took advantage of the opportunity to change him into some clean, hospital-issued pajamas.

Ben was so excited about the pancake breakfast that he asked, "Can I ride my pole to the party?" He had seen one of the other children "riding the pole" several days earlier. The IV pole is tall and has a rather large, wheeled base for support. Otherwise, the pole would constantly be tipping over. To "ride the pole," the child straddles the pole while standing on the bottom ring above the wheels, holds on, and rides as the parent pushes the pole down the hall. It's great fun.

"Of course you can ride the pole," I said. "Let's go eat!"

The sudden enthusiasm and renewed spirit in Ben was more than uplifting to all who knew him. I'm convinced that his renewed energy was a gift from above (and from Mickey Mouse pancakes). The morning was terrific.

We watched with huge smiles as Dr. Salman and his two young children made Mickey Mouse-shaped pancakes out of Bisquick for all of us. They decorated Mickey's face with chocolate chips for the eyes, a strawberry for the nose, and a big whipped cream smile. Patients, parents, and staff were able to join in on the fun. Dr. Salman and his children made the kids feel like kings and queens, and they made us parents feel pretty special, too.

All of those precious bald children lugging around their loaded IV poles sat around a long table and laughed, cheered, and ate. And they ate a lot. As parents, we watched with hearts full of joy. It was the kind of joy you feel when you are completely surprised as you open a special, unexpected gift—a warm and fulfilling joy so intense that it fills your heart and soul.

That's just how it was in our little hospital in Florida. We were receiving state-of-the-art chemotherapy protocols, we were receiving exceptionally compassionate care, and we were home. Every cancer program in the world has its positive and negative attributes. Some of these places are very large, and some are very small. Some see their

Sandie Klassen

kids as an eight-digit number, and others see their kids as family. Maybe it is all in what you make of it individually; I don't know. But for us, it made all the difference in the world to not have to be completely uprooted and find ourselves alone in a strange city when we had everything near home. So, to this day, I am so glad that we stayed.

10

Germs

We were only able to spend four days at home at the beginning of the new year, 2001. Ben woke up crying at 2:00 a.m. His cry was intense, as if he had just been burned with boiling hot water. I rushed to his side to find him in his bed completely soaked in sweat. His pillowcase was wet, his sheets were wet, his pajamas were wet, and his hair looked as if he had stuck it under the faucet of the bathroom sink. Having been awakened abruptly to race to Ben's side, I found myself breathing heavily.

"Ben, what's the matter?" I asked through my slight panic.

"I don't know," he said crying. "I feel terrible and my head hurts."

One of the nurses had told me how important it was going to be to have a good thermometer in the house because we would need to check Ben's temperature frequently. I had purchased an electronic ear thermometer earlier that day. At first I was hesitant to make the investment, but as I stood in front of the thermometer section at the drugstore, I finally decided that the nurse was right. A good thermometer would make everything easier. To get a three-year-old to keep the old-fashioned mercury thermometer under his tongue for three minutes was nearly impossible, and the armpit trick was never successful because of giggles. Even though I loved the giggles, they did get in the way of the business of taking a temperature. I was glad to have the technology of the digital thermometer at my fingertips when this evening's events arose.

I was fairly certain of the thermometer's reading before I pressed the plastic tip into his right ear, but I took the reading anyway. Ben, without a doubt, had a fever. After the high-pitched beep sounded, I looked to the digital screen and read 103.1. Chuck was already awake and making his way to Ben's bedroom when I called for his help.

At one time in my life, I swear that a freight train could have gone through my bedroom, and I would have slept right through it. Since the children were born, my sleep pattern had changed significantly, and now I was a fairly light sleeper. After Ben was diagnosed, an even more remarkable change occurred with my sensitivity to sounds in the night; I don't think I could have slept through a breeze rustling the curtains on my window. Chuck was the same, so when Ben began crying, Chuck and I were instantly awakened. As soon as we saw what was happening, we looked at each other. Both of us already knew exactly what to do. I grabbed the phone.

Our orders were to call Dr. Salman, day or night, if we had any questions, problems, or even slight concerns. Furthermore, we were specifically instructed to call the doctor if Ben had a temperature of 100.2 or above. The doctor explained that although this seemed like a low and insignificant temperature reading, it was, in fact, an indication of potentially serious trouble. Anytime a person has any sort of hardware or other foreign matter in the body, bacteria tend to migrate toward the site of that object. Therefore, after Ben's new port was put into his chest, the likelihood of an infection settling at that spot greatly increased, and we were directed to take no chances.

"With a temperature of even 100.2, you pick up the phone to call me. I do not care what time it is," Doctor Salman had said as we left the hospital. So, I quickly dialed the number that I had already committed to memory during our first discharge interview just four days earlier.

A woman's voice picked up on the other end of the line. "Hello, Dr. Salman's answering service. How may I help you?" Her voice was alert and cheerful as if it were 2:00 p.m. in the afternoon.

"My son is a patient of Dr. Salman's, and I think he is very sick. Can you get the doctor for me, please?" I asked while trying to keep my voice calm and clear.

She asked for Ben's name and my name. She then paused for what seemed like an eternity. The silence was deafening and thoughts began to race through my mind. There was certainly no way that the doctor had told her something depressing about Ben's condition. That would have been a breach of patient confidentiality. On the other hand, why did she seem to go on alert when I mentioned Ben's name? My thoughts were spinning as fast as the end of a washing machine cycle.

I'm sure now that she did not intentionally hesitate in the conversation. There was probably no pause in the conversation at all;

A Test of Faith

it was all in my mind. The woman taking the call was most likely writing down the information I had given and completing the necessary paperwork on her end.

When she finally continued, she asked, "What seems to be the problem?"

I told her about the sweating, the fever, and the shrill cry. I asked her to please hurry and have the doctor call me. She reassured me that it would not be long before he would do just that.

I was so thankful that our oncologist was considerate of the panic that frequently formed in the minds of us parents. I barely had time to return to Ben's room, where I found him rocking in his daddy's arms, when the phone in the kitchen began to ring. I raced back to answer it.

"Hi, Dr. Salman," I answered a bit out of breath. I usually answer the phone with a simple "hello," but obviously I already knew it was the doctor who was calling. No one else was going to be calling at 2:00 a.m. anyway.

"Hello, Mrs. Klassen. Yes, this is Dr. Salman," he said. He asked exactly what was going on with Ben, so I explained in detail. The conversation had only lasted about thirty seconds when he said, "You need to bring him into the hospital immediately. Go directly up to the floor, and I will meet you there."

Chuck called his mom, who was on our list of caregivers for Dana should an emergency such as this occur. Much to our relief, his mother, Vonita, who was also startled from a sound sleep, said that she would be right over. She managed to get to our house within twenty minutes.

We were admitted back into the hospital by 3:00 a.m. As soon as we arrived, the nurse had the room ready for us, and the IV pole was set up at the side of the bed with fluid bags marked with Ben's name already hung. Several yards of the plastic tubing had been untangled and were draped over the top of the pole. There was a tray sitting on the bedside table that was full of medical supplies used for drawing and collecting blood, and there were four small bottles standing upright on the corner of the tray. The bottles reminded me of the old Coke bottles we used to get when we were in the old town pharmacies on vacations when I was a kid. There were at least three small glass tubes with differently colored caps lying in a row beside the bottles, lots of alcohol packets, Betadine packets, and, of course, the needle.

The nurse was very calm when we arrived. I was holding Ben in my arms, and his sweaty head was resting on my left shoulder. The nurse must have registered the fear on my face because she spoke first. "Everything will be fine, Sandie. Try to relax."

I looked at her and just nodded.

Before the nurse could draw the blood cultures, Ben's port first had to be accessed. It was only the second time that this had been done, and the first time proved to be more than a traumatic procedure for him. He was very scared and just hated the thought of the needle.

"Accessing a port" meant that the nurse would put a needle through the skin into the small disc below the skin. The needle had a ten-inch hose attached to it and a cap on the end of that hose. After the needle was safely placed, it was then secured with tape. A sticky, clear plastic, square bandage was used as a dressing so that the nurses could always see the integrity of the needle site. If redness, swelling, or draining occurred near the needle, it would have to come out immediately.

We were given a small tube of cream at discharge and were told to always have a tube of this cream handy. The medicine was actually called EMLA, which was a blend of Prilocaine and Lidocaine, that worked to numb Ben's skin. It was a great topical numbing agent and worked superbly to take away the pain of the needle stick, but unfortunately, it did nothing for the anxiety in the small boy's mind. We called the medicine our "magic cream," and in the car on the way to the hospital, Ben let me put a small dollop of this cream onto his port. I covered the white blob that resembled regular body lotion with a clear bandage called Tegaderm. After about twenty minutes, the skin under the cream would be blanched white and theoretically it would be numb.

This was the first time we had used our magic cream, and, as such, my first try in getting the Tegaderm patch onto the skin was a flop. The two edges touched each other and immediately stuck together. It was impossible to pull the edges apart, so I just wadded the sticky mess into a ball and threw it onto the backseat floor of the car. My second try was successful, and we had the cream covered and hopefully doing its job.

Before the nurse could begin her work on Ben, I sat on the bed with him on my lap facing away from me. He was so frightened to see the nurse prepare to work with the port that he squeezed both of my hands so tightly that my fingers began to throb. At first he was very quiet, but then he started whimpering. Soon he began to cry with intensity as tears streamed down his cheeks.

"Please no," he spoke through his sobs. "Don't do this to me! Please, Mommy, don't let them do this. I hate this!"

To hear his pleading just about killed me. I was even more alarmed when I realized that the dampness on my thigh was from Ben urinating. He was so scared that he had wet his pants. I did not say anything to him except that I loved him and that we were going to be ok. I told him to ask Jesus to sit on the bed beside us, and that is precisely what Ben did. "Please, Jesus, will you hold my hand?" were his exact words. I started shaking, and was finding it difficult to hold back my tears. I knew, though, that I had to be strong. I knew that my strength would somehow be a comfort to Ben, but I wanted more than anything to fall apart, take Ben into my arms, and run away from all of this. I wanted to put a stop to it all and make Ben happy and healthy again. Unfortunately, we had no choice but to proceed.

The port was accessed in a matter of a few minutes, and the blood cultures were drawn from the intravenous line that was now in place. When all of the bottles and tubes were filled with dark red blood, they were tagged with stickers with Ben's name and account number and sent to the lab. The nurse then hooked up the tubing that was hanging over the IV pole, and soon Ben was receiving fluids. He had stopped crying and was now getting tired, all of which was a huge relief and comfort to me. When Ben's eyes became droopy and his body went limp, I laid him in the bed, pulled the white blanket up to his chin, and placed his big, yellow, Winnie the Pooh bear beside him. I was glad that Chuck had thrown the stuffed animal into the car at the last minute. Dr. Salman told us that if we were to be admitted for a fever, it was very likely that the admission would last at least three to five days. Ben and Pooh Bear were a close-knit pair. If Pooh wasn't there, Ben wouldn't be content to be there, either.

The tremendous emotional strain had exhausted our little boy, and he was soon fast asleep. I was relieved that he was finally comfortable but was still worried about what was happening. As it turned out, our stay lasted a full seven days, and it seemed like forever until we were told we could go back home again.

Our initial schedule on this protocol had us home for two weeks to rest and recover before returning for the second round of chemotherapy. We had just spent seven of those days back in the hospital for the infection, so we were left with just one short week of home time. We enjoyed the week as best we could considering we were still at the clinic every other day for checkups, but all in all, it was good healthy time together as a family. Ben could not understand that this was to be our routine for the next five months. Chuck and I could not accept the idea very well, either.

While someone receives chemotherapy as a treatment for cancer, the immune system takes a beating. The body is working so hard to process the foreign, toxic chemicals of the chemotherapy that the white blood cells take a hit and cannot keep up with their job of warding off infection. In addition, many of the white cells are beat up and virtually destroyed by the chemotherapy itself, so it is very common for the patient to develop a fever, rash, or infection, or to just plain feel awful while they are receiving treatment.

The development of a rash, fever, infection, or lethargy can also be a sign of a very serious emergency in an already sick body. Part of the white blood cell count that the cancer patient gets to know well is called the ANC. The white blood cell count is differentiated in the lab and broken down into its components. That means the lab can take a small sample of the blood and determine the percentages of each type of white blood cell in the sample. This data is very important as it can give information on what is happening in the body. For example, the doctor can get an idea about the risk of a viral or bacterial infection, toxicity to the chemicals, tissue damage, or many other problems just from the breakdown of the white blood cells. So, when the lab determines the individual percentages of the components of the cells, the resultant number is termed the ANC, or absolute neutrophil count.

When this ANC drops to 500, the patient's defense system is getting pretty weak. An ANC below 500 is an indication that the patient is at a severe risk for infection. If the ANC drops to zero, there is essentially no working immune system at all, and the person is at total risk for any and all infections. If the ANC is at zero, it is almost guaranteed that the patient will get very sick, and this is a very critical and dangerous time during the treatment course. Because the patient cannot defend against the infection, the infection will continue to grow until it takes over the entire body and the person dies. Immediate medical intervention is imperative. Ben's ANC when we were initially discharged from the hospital was only 20.

A Test of Faith

Dr. Salman later told me that because of Ben's low ANC, he was not surprised that Ben developed a fever when we were discharged. He was relatively certain that we would be calling late one night, just as we did.

Our bodies are designed to defend against a multitude of bacteria, viruses, molds, funguses, and every other existing microorganism. The fact that most people rarely get sick is simply amazing. I watched a special on *Nova* one time and was really shocked by the microscopic study of our world. Germs are everywhere. The unseen world that goes on around us is fascinating. Our world is so much more detailed and complicated than we could ever imagine unless we took the time to study the details. It makes me think about how powerfully creative and how in tune with detail God is. He wants everything about this world to be organized and painstakingly meticulous. My knowledge of germs proved to be valuable now that Ben was vulnerable to them.

Chuck and I kept a schedule where one of us stayed at home with Dana and the other stayed with Ben at the hospital. We rotated every other night. While we were there in the hospital with him, there was never a minute of rest. It was amazing how busy a little boy could keep a parent, especially a sick little boy. I did not mind one bit staying busy to help him.

On my night off, I was able to recharge my energy and spirit so that when I was on duty, I was ready to answer to Ben's every need. That was all I could do. Most of the time I wished I could do more—such as throw up for him, take the shot for him, or basically take the disease for him—but I couldn't. The best I could do was pray for him, encourage him, be positive, and help him with his needs. I also needed to listen to him. He had things that he wanted to say and questions he needed answered.

Some of our conversations were more mature than I could have ever imagined between an adult and a three-year-old boy. I often had to sit in my car for just a few minutes before going into the hospital for shift change. There, I would pray for a good night, dead cancer cells, and a cure, and mostly I would pray for strength for me and for Ben. I prayed for whatever comforting words God thought Ben needed to hear from me, and I prayed for every bit of energy that I could get to be the best caregiver in the world to my baby. I had to bounce into the hospital with a smile and all the enthusiasm I could muster, and I felt that I needed to enter Ben's room like a ray of sunshine. I don't know why I put all of this pressure on myself, but I just sensed that it was important. I needed so desperately for him to know that life was still good and worth a good fight. I had to bring him joy and some laughter during this awful time. I had to let him know by my actions and attitude that this battle with cancer was ok. This was merely one of life's challenges, one we could conquer. I had to believe that everything would soon be normal again. I had to bring Ben peace and hope. Maybe I was doing it for me, too.

Our routine was to spend a lot of time in the hospital. If we were admitted, it was to take seven days' worth of a course of chemotherapy, or a dose of antibiotics and a watchful eye. That was what happened on this very dreadful night when Ben woke up soaked with sweat and fever. Ben had an infection of some sort. Nothing spectacular showed up in all the tubes of blood sent to the lab, so he was treated with many antibiotic doses and watched closely for any significant changes or deterioration of health. The doctor and nurses circled around him constantly to be sure that his status did not change. They watched, examined, and studied his blood day and night.

When we were discharged from that week's "fever stay," we went directly into our "out of the hospital" program, which meant that we still went to the hospital every day or every other day. The way I figure it, we were still in the hospital; we just didn't have to sleep there.

The daily visits to the clinic (or, if we were lucky, every other day) were used to monitor Ben as closely as possible without the constant twenty-four-hour, around-the-clock expense and time of an actual admission. In the clinic, which contained the infamous blue exam room, Ben was given his very frequent physical examinations and then had his blood tested. Depending on the results of the blood studies, he received any transfusions that might be required. If the red blood cells dropped below 8.0, Ben was transfused with packed red cells. To have a transfusion of red cells took about four hours. If the platelets dropped to 10.0, then they were transfused, too, but this procedure took only about fifteen minutes and was usually quick and easy. If he did not require any blood products, we could be out of there in about three hours. If he did need something for his blood, we were in the clinic anywhere from five to seven hours.

A Test of Faith

Even though the time in the clinic made for a long day, it was entirely refreshing to know that we could go home together at night. We would have dinner together at the kitchen table, play games, read books, and tuck each other into bed with a lot of hugs, kisses, and prayers. We were very thankful to be together, the four of us, like a normal family.

While I was at the hospital with Ben, either during an inpatient stay or the long days at the clinic, I spent a lot of time sitting close to him reading books. When we were admitted, I went back and forth to the nurse's station, again and again, to find a movie to watch or a game to play. His favorite movie became *My Dog Skip*, but he always called it "*Skip Dog*."

"Let's watch '*Skip Dog*,' Mommy."

"Again??" I'd say.

When I felt a little stir crazy, and Ben was up to it, I would locate one of the many red wagons donated to the ward and spend about ten minutes wiping it down with alcohol and other cleaning solutions the nurses provided. When I was content that the wagon was germ free, I padded the bottom with a pillow and prepared a cozy little setup. Then Ben, wrapped in a blanket, was lifted into it. I quickly learned how to pull the wagon and the IV pole at the same time without taking out my heels. We would walk slowly, doing laps around the second floor of the hospital. Each floor's hallway was designed as a balcony that overlooked the beautiful atrium below. It was always a very slow walk, around and around and around.

Ben loved to be out in the halls and see the activity. It was such a nice change from the four walls of his room for both of us. It was refreshing to see people other than the nurses and doctors, too. Ben would gently wave at the old folks sitting in the easy chairs waiting for appointments to whatever test or treatment they had going. They always smiled at Ben and his skinny body and bald head. I sometimes wondered what was going through their minds. On occasion, I would stop so that they could talk to Ben, and they would say things like, "Good morning, little fellow," "Hi, champ," and "You look great today, young man." You could see their hearts melt as we went by. I was thankful for their gifts of compassion. I always had to wipe a tear from my own eye as I walked away. It was so emotional to see how Ben was touching all of these lives.

Before I knew it, people were greeting my little boy by his name. The greetings became "Good morning, little Ben," and "You are looking great today, Ben." I still do not know how so many people learned of Ben's name. To this day, I do not think they have forgotten about him, and I certainly have not forgotten about them. I am so thankful for their bright smiles and compassion for us. They made me feel as if everything was going to be ok. They gave me so much strength to go another lap.

I always packed the pink bucket in the wagon. The bucket was the usual square tub that is found in every hospital supply room and on every oncology patient's bedside table. We never went anywhere without the bucket. Two of them, actually. As soon as Ben felt the need to vomit, he would yell, "YIKES, BUCKET!!" I had to move, and quick! He would vomit, or worse, dry heave for several minutes. After the expulsion, my job was to wipe his mouth, replace the vomit-filled bucket with the ready clean one, go rinse out the messy one, and run back to his side to begin round two. Sometimes this lasted for ten minutes, and sometimes it would last for a full hour or more. I always felt so bad for him.

If the nauseous feeling or vomiting ever got out of control, which it did often, the nurses would be right at our side with anti-emetic medicines. Zofran became our favorite drug for a while, and we called for it often. It was a fragile, white piece of paper that we had to put under Ben's tongue and let it dissolve. It was like cotton candy in the way it melted, but it offered none of the fun of cotton candy. You are supposed to enjoy this melt-in-your-mouth candy at a fair or amusement park, and this place was nothing of the sort.

I wished often that it would soon be time to go have fun. I told Ben that we would go to Disney World and get real cotton candy someday soon. I knew deep down that we would be able to go sometime. We had to. Every kid needs to enjoy an amusement park now and then.

So, during those sleepless nights I watched my bald baby lying there, throwing up, receiving medicines and more medicines, watching "*Skip Dog*," and having scans. He was suffering and so was I. I often had to step out of the room to regain my composure. I would lean my head against the wall and try to take deep breaths. I tried to stay standing, even though my legs were crumbling beneath me. I tried to control my shaking hands and desperately tried to stay calm.

My heart would be racing and the tears would want to fall, every minute of each of these days. All I could think was, "Why, Lord? Why couldn't this just be happening to me and not Ben? Why, Lord?"

11

Choosing Duke

Even though we were focused on Ben day to day, we had to look ahead to the next stage of his treatment. We made the decision about a month prior to surgery that we would take Ben to Duke University Medical Center in Durham, North Carolina, for the bone marrow transplant portion of the protocol. We searched and studied the different transplant programs at several institutions around the country. We even looked at what was offered in Europe, as we were not close minded to going to any place that could save our son's life.

Chuck spent hours on the Internet reading about various institutions and their programs. We printed pages and pages from the Web and read about patient-to-nurse ratios, doctors on staff, specialties, facilities, housing in the area, location, research articles coming out of the labs, highlights of expert procedures at the place, and any other facts that came across the computer screen. We could not find any information on the computer specific to the outcomes of bone marrow transplants on kids with neuroblastoma even from the pioneer of transplants for kids with this cancer, Robert Seger, M.D. of the Children's Hospital of Los Angeles, so we had to continue with our study.

We made phone calls to doctors we knew who were experts in pediatrics, genetics, and neurology and even contacted a head and neck surgeon. We made phone calls within Florida and out to Minnesota, Kentucky, Georgetown University in Washington, D.C., and Illinois. We talked to anyone who might know anything about the reputations and abilities of any transplant unit across the world. We asked our neighbors from Scotland and Germany what they knew. We wanted to talk to anyone who might have had some insight as to where we should go for this most important and critical step in our treatment. We talked to other people who had been through a bone marrow transplant and asked them of their experiences. We looked up information and ratings of hospitals in *Newsweek, U.S. News and World Report*, and even glanced at a *Consumer Report,* which wasn't helpful at all. Looking back now, I know it was silly to even think to look there; *Consumer Report* may be a good source for shopping for cars, washing machines, and televisions, but not an oncology and transplant program. However, we were a little frantic and searched through anything we could get our hands on.

Choosing the right transplant unit for Ben was really a big decision for us. As always, I also prayed and I prayed often. We needed direction and then security in knowing that we'd made the right decision. We spent a lot of time drilling Dr. Salman for his best advice and gut feelings about where the best place would be for Ben to be transplanted. We talked to some other doctors in the Ft. Myers area, too. Most were adult oncologists, but some had valuable advice for a pediatric case.

After weeks of reading, calling, talking, searching, and praying, we finally decided that we wanted to take Benjamin to Duke University. The transplant unit there seemed to be everything that we wanted for our son. We wanted people who had performed countless transplants. We wanted our type of transplant and our diagnosis to be well known to them. We liked the fact that the team at Duke had transplanted thousands of kids and that people from literally all over the world were waiting as long as they could to admit their children onto this unit. We were sure that their transplant team's experience over the years would mean that they had to have seen it all. They certainly could manage any complication that might arise because chances were that they had seen almost any complication possible.

Duke was heavily involved in research, so we figured they would have access to breaking news and information coming out of the labs. They might know about some probable research outcomes that were literally still growing in test tubes, including information that had not even had a chance yet to be shared with the COG. Maybe they had access to drugs still in clinical trials with the FDA that had not yet been approved but were getting close.

Duke University had one doctor with a passion for the cancer called neuroblastoma. He had spent hours in his laboratory studying this disease, and it was the focus of his research. It was reassuring to know that with all the many cancers that could affect children, this doctor took a special interest in and dedicated his time to only neuroblastoma. If we had the opportunity to work with a man who had a total and complete passion for Ben's disease and was dedicating his life to curing this monster, it made perfect sense to have him in charge of our son. The other doctors around the world were most likely extremely talented, too, but they may have been more focused on leukemia, rhabdosarcoma, or lymphoma. We had neuroblastoma, so we needed a neuroblastoma specialist.

In addition to the medical center and the transplant unit at Duke, the rest of the information that we gathered about that institution was reassuring to us, too. The overall reputation of the university was excellent. It was elite. It had educated and graduated some people who had made very significant contributions to our world.

Because Duke was so prestigious, I sensed on one visit to the campus an attitude that was a bit pompous, but the staff were success driven, and we needed nothing less than perfect success on this transplant. The idea of taking the last step of our cancer treatment at Duke seemed right for us. Our gut feeling was that this was the place for Benjamin to be cured.

A remarkable woman named Dr. Joanne Kurtzberg, M.D., led the pediatric transplant team at Duke. She was an unpretentious yet brilliant physician who had set up a state-of-the-art program for allogeneic and autologous bone marrow transplants. Ben was in need of an autologous transplant, and Dr. Kurtzberg and her team were more than experts in dealing with such a medical procedure.

I learned that an allogeneic transplant is when the patient receives bone marrow cells from a donor whose genetic makeup perfectly matches the patient's, or comes as close to perfect as possible. Most people believe that a match from a sibling or parent would come closest to a patient's genetic makeup, but in reality, a sibling match is relatively rare and a parent match is even less likely. A sibling will only have about a 35 percent chance of genetically matching the patient.

We had Dana tested for her compatibility with Ben just in case because clean bone marrow cells from a person who never had cancer would have been ideal for Ben. But, as statistics predicted, Dana was only a four-out-of-six match. A match that low was too risky and basically impossible to do. If we had used Dana's poorly matched bone marrow, Ben's body would have perceived the marrow as a foreign material, and his body would have tried to attack and destroy it. He most certainly would have had a potentially deadly complication called "graft-versus-host disease." We opted not to search a bone marrow bank because neuroblastoma was equally suited to be treated by the other type of transplant called "autologous."

Had I known of Dr. Kurtzberg's discovery of the use of umbilical cord blood for transplantation when Ben was born, I could have had the umbilical cord that connected me to Ben reserved for an emergency such as this. Quite possibly, that blood would have been pure of any cancer cells, and, of course, it would have been an identical match to Ben. Unfortunately, the option of saving that blood was never offered to me when Ben was born, and I knew nothing of it to ask.

Dr. Kurtzberg discovered that the blood remaining in the umbilical cord after mother and baby are separated has wonderful medical potential. Usually this blood is discarded with the rest of the placenta and cord. Dr Kurtzberg, however, pioneered the idea to preserve this cord blood and then use it for transplantation for kids with cancer or hematological disorders. The idea was remarkable, and it already has saved many, many lives. I understand that hospitals all over the country now have banks of this cord blood stored for those in need of a transplant. This woman is truly one of God's greatest vehicles. Her work, and that of her team, continues to pave the way to curing pediatric cancer through transplants. Not all cancers need the allogeneic transplant, however, and as I mentioned, Ben was in need of the autologous option.

An autologous transplant is possible if the disease afflicting the bone marrow is temporarily gone (such as in complete remission), or if the cancer type does not affect the bone marrow in the first place. If you think of the bone marrow as the factory for producing the blood cells, then if the factory is clean, it can produce cells that will function perfectly in the body. However, if something unusual, such as a solid cancer tumor, invades the body, the cells go haywire. If the factory itself is malfunctioning, then it will manufacture bad cells in the first place.

It's kind of like an automobile factory. If the factory in Michigan makes perfect cars, then all is well unless there is a huge pile-up on the expressway. The cars will then be damaged. Otherwise, it is safe to conclude that when the car comes off the assembly line, it will work perfectly. However, if there is a glitch in the factory and something in every car is produced defectively, when the car is out on the expressway, it will still be defective no matter what environmental influences arise. In the case of neuroblastoma, the factory is perfect, but when the cells are put into the blood stream, they are injured by the tumor. With a cancer such as leukemia, however, the factory is messed up in the first place, so the cells being put out into the blood stream are already defective.

With the autologous transplant, there is no need to search for a genetic match from a donor bank because in this case, the patient's own healthy bone marrow cells are harvested from the patient's own body. The cells are then tested to be certain that they are, in fact, cancer free. They are cleaned (or purged), preserved, and then stored in a freezer. Later, at transplant time, these clean, pure, healthy, working cells are re-infused back into the patient.

Including Dr. Kurtzberg, there were five doctors on the transplant team at Duke University. The doctor to be in charge of our case was Dr. Driscoll. He was the one who specialized in neuroblastoma, and his entire career was dedicated to the research and cure of this particular type of cancer. As soon as we met him, we felt his passion. When we talked to him about his lab or his patients, he lit up like a kid in a candy store. He wanted to tell us everything. He told us about his slides, his latest thoughts, and what he was doing with them. He told about the exciting discoveries he had made in his lab and those on the brink. He also had a heart. He wanted the right things in life, and he seemed to have his priorities straight. He truly was a gifted man, and we were grateful that he shared his talents.

Equally talented was his assistant, Tracy Kelly. Even though Tracy was not a doctor (her degree was Pediatric Nurse Practitioner), she was tough and even kept Dr. Driscoll in line. She assisted with taking Ben's history and with his physical examination. In addition, she was the organizer. She was probably the key to Dr. Driscoll's sanity, for it was her structure that kept the program rolling for us. I contacted her again and again to schedule appointments and arrange our follow-up visits. She was incredibly busy, as was the entire staff, but she always took the time to know her patients, and she knew Ben well. I would call her and leave a voice mail message actually spelling our last name:

"Hi, Tracy, this is Ben's mom, Sandie Klassen…that's K-L-A-S-S-E-N…"

She would crack up at the message and reply by always spelling back my name. Her sense of humor always lightened even the most tense of moments and helped us feel loved by our Duke team. So, between Tracy and Dr. Driscoll, we would be well cared for. We were in exceptionally capable hands, and we were relieved to have found them.

It was important that we had decided on Duke University prior to the surgery because the tumor that was to be surgically removed from Ben was to be sent to Duke so that Dr. Driscoll could study it, dissect it, and explore every aspect of it. We wanted him to completely understand the histology of Ben's particular tumor.

It wasn't until April that the CT scan finally showed some definition and differentiation between the tumor and the neighboring structures in Ben's abdomen. Finally, it looked as if it was time to cut that disgusting, pathetic, no-good ball of life-threatening garbage out of there, and I was relieved. For four months now it had seemed absurd to be doing aggressive treatments with chemotherapy when the source of the disease was still present, not only existing, but stealing nutrients and life from Ben so that it could continue to flourish and thrive. I understood that it was far too dangerous to try to go in earlier to remove the tumor because there were so many tentacles reaching off of this glob of wickedness and wrapping themselves around vital structures in my boy's belly. Nevertheless, I still had a hard time accepting that we were truly fighting hard from the outside while this demon was still fighting to exist on the inside.

"The most recent CT scan indicates that the tumor has shrunk to less than half of its original size," said Dr. Salman. "It looks like it is time to start thinking about having it surgically removed."

I was overjoyed when the doctor gave us this news, but I was also worried. I wanted the tumor, the thief, out of my son, but I understood that abdominal surgery was very complicated, and there were tremendous risks that we would have to face. There was a chance of losing the kidney upon which the tumor was sitting. There could be problems simply in removing the tumor that could result in many complications, including infection, excessive blood loss or even hemorrhaging, or a reaction to the anesthesia that could cause Ben to die. The thought of someone opening up his little tummy and digging around for at least four hours was unsettling, but it was time, and I was ready.

We had Ben checked in and ready for surgery by 5:30 on a Thursday morning. We really did not have to be at the hospital until 6:00 a.m., but we were worried about traffic. Also, neither Chuck nor I could sleep, so we had Ben at the hospital much earlier than our scheduled time. We paced the floors of the empty waiting room early that day. We watched as the sun slowly rose and began to filter into the room through the large glass windowpanes. We watched as people, old and young, slowly came in and registered for their procedures. I wondered why they were there. I'm positive that they wondered about us, too.

Ben sat quietly on the vinyl chair. He did not say much but did not look worried, either. He was comfortable and still very sleepy. He was tired this early morning, as he usually did not awaken for at least another two hours. This was still supposed to be dreamtime for him.

When it was finally our turn to proceed back to the surgery pre-op area, we all stood up and walked together. With Ben between us, Chuck and I each took one of his hands. We passed through a narrow corridor and made our way into a holding area where each patient station was curtained off for privacy. There were several stretchers lined in a row, and at the end of each was a square piece of paper taped to the bed. Written in a black marker was Ben's name. Below his name in red was the surgeon's name.

The area was very busy with dozens of people, all dressed in green scrubs and surgical caps, moving quickly around to several stations. The lights were fluorescent and very bright; the sounds were consistent with the hospital world with pumps beeping, pagers ringing, and everyone speaking the foreign language of medical terminology. Most unsettling was the smell. The antiseptic, anesthetic, intense hospital smell was everywhere. Unlike baking bread, which provokes an immediate feeling of home and security, this smell triggered tension and uncertainty.

Ben sat on my lap on the gurney just as he had for that first CT scan. He was shaking in my arms.

"Are you cold, honey? Do you want a blanket?" I asked.

"No, Mommy, I'm scared."

Ben's response was more than I was ready to handle. A lump formed in my throat. Oh God, honey, I am too, I thought.

"Everything will be ok," I said. "Jesus will be with you the entire time, and everything will be ok. I promise."

A Test of Faith

I did not say another word because I did not know what to say. I was afraid that Ben would sense the fear in my voice, so I just kept quiet. I held Ben close. When it was finally his turn, the doctor came over, pushed a sedative drug into Ben's IV, asked us to sign a paper, and then left. He was not very talkative, but neither was I. I just wanted this tumor out, and I wanted it out now.

It took the Ft. Myers pediatric surgeon four hours, just as expected, to complete the operation. He was very meticulous in his work, and he took his time to minimize any blood loss. Word has it that the only blood lost in the surgery was what was soaked up in a dozen gauze sponges. The surgeon was incredible. He did everything that he was supposed to do and saved Ben's kidney, too. His hands were gifted, and I was both happy and relieved. I also felt lucky that he was near our home in Ft. Myers, Florida, to work on my son. The work he did in the operating room that morning was truly miraculous.

While the surgery was taking place, something else miraculous was happening in my life. I couldn't concentrate, couldn't eat, and couldn't keep any of my thoughts straight, so once again I turned to God. I did not know what to say that would not be the same begging or pleading for safety and health for Ben, so I opened the Bible beside me on the waiting room table. I blindly opened the hard cover book because I really did not know what I was looking for. I was just hoping to read something that would keep me busy. The scripture that immediately caught my eye on the page I opened read: ***"For I will restore health unto thee, and I will heal thee, saith the Lord."*** (Jeremiah 30:17).

A rush of adrenaline flowed up and down my spine and my arms, and it made my heart flutter. This had happened to me only one other time in my life, and I was not used to God being so direct with me. I looked up and around the room, but no one was paying any attention to me. Chuck had left earlier to find a cup of coffee, and the other folks in the waiting area were reading their magazines, watching CNN on the television, or napping. No one had any idea of what had just miraculously happened in my moment of prayer. I slowly closed the Bible and rested my hand gently on the book. My index finger slowly traced the embossed emblem on the center of the front cover, and I felt an overwhelming sense of relief and peace.

I wished everyone in the whole world could experience something like this. Deep down I knew that everyone could. It was free for the taking; you just had to ask, and I was so glad that I did. It was at least the second time in my life that prayers had been answered so emphatically, immediately, and without reservation, so now I was convinced about the truth of the Bible and about the truth of God. I felt protected. I knew that I could never get through this crisis on my own, and I was so thankful for Jesus being by my side to comfort me and give me strength.

Nothing in my life mattered more to me than Ben and Dana, but equal to that love were God's promises to me of heaven. I was so thankful that Jesus continued to forgive me and love me and care about me simply because of Grace.

The gray-haired lady in the pink smock behind the reception desk called my name. She may have called it a few times, I'm not sure, but finally she got my attention. When I looked up at her, she smiled and said I could go back to the recovery room. Ben was asking for his mommy.

12

The Central Line

Overall, Ben recovered nicely from the surgery to remove the tumor, and our prayers were being answered one after another. Strange things continued to happen to us, though, and while Ben was recovering from the surgery, one more encounter with God really opened our eyes.

Ben woke up in the middle of the night screaming. When Chuck rushed to his side, he was sitting up in his hospital bed and crying because of the intense pain in his belly. He complained that he could not lie down, and he asked if Chuck would please help him.

Curious, Chuck said, "Sure." But then he asked Ben, "How did you get up to a sitting position?"

"Jesus helped me," Ben replied.

Chuck reported that he was not able to go back to sleep the rest of that night. He sat at Ben's side and watched the boy sleep. Every so often he looked around the room and just watched to see if anything odd was happening.

At daybreak, Chuck called me. He woke me from a deep sleep to tell me what had happened. I was speechless. I wonder even now why Ben would ever say something like that unless it was really true. Why else in the middle of the night would a little three-year-old boy answer his dad's question with the words, "Jesus helped me"? I truly believe God was with us through every step of this journey.

While Ben was under anesthesia for the tumor removal, the surgeon inserted a Hickman catheter into a large vein in the right side of Ben's chest just above his heart. The double hose, or "double lumen," as they called it, was really just a flexible tube that was necessary for a bone marrow transplant. This tube would allow the doctors and staff to administer drugs and blood products to Ben. Also, it would be used to withdraw the hundreds of blood samples that would be required during the course of treatments for transplant. The hose would be great because it would prevent the need to insert needles into Ben's arms or hands. To try to put all of the chemicals and medicines into a regular vein in the arm or back of the hand would never work because the vein would most likely collapse. Using the mediport would not work, either, because of the volume of various fluids and the number of different substances that had to go in all at once. So, we signed the necessary paperwork, and the central line was placed in Ben's chest.

I was not at all sure what to expect of this catheter as I had never before seen one. The first sight of it made me anxious and doubtful that I would ever be able to manage its care. When I lifted up Ben's hospital gown, I saw a thick, white, long rubbery tube about one-quarter inch in diameter coming straight out of his tiny chest. I tried not to act shocked.

"Wow, Ben! Look at this. Isn't this neat? This is your new garden hose."

Ben looked down at his chest and then up at me. His expression was not at all enthusiastic. "Why do I have to have this?" he asked.

I explained that it would help us at Duke. "No one will ever have to poke you in the arm again if we have this new garden hose," I told him.

"Why can't we just keep using my port?" he asked.

I was once again amazed at his intellect. I told him that the port would still be used, but we were going to need these hoses because Duke had really special medicine that would get rid of the bad guy cells once and for all. He seemed to understand my lame explanation, so we left it at that.

The Hickman catheter looked fascinating but frightening. I was awed once again by advances in medical technology. I had left the waiting room with an attitude of stoutheartedness after my answered prayer. I greeted Ben in the recovery room feeling like Atlas. I could carry the entire world on my shoulders. Suddenly, however, after looking at Ben's new central line, I felt instantly humbled and even powerless. I wondered again if I could go on.

About five inches below the tube's exit from the chest, the hose split into two sections, each another eight inches in length. These hoses hung down almost to Ben's waist. The catheter was made for an adult, but because none had ever been designed for pediatric patients, this was the smallest model available to use on Ben. The long rubber tubing was loosely looped so that it could be taped to his skin in a safe position about his waistline. At the end of each hose was a clear cap that prevented air or anything else from entering. The caps were also used to inject medicines into the tubing, where they would travel up the hose and finally run directly into Ben's heart.

Prior to surgery, the nursing staff on the floor told me that I would be responsible for caring for Ben's central line when we were at home. The whole idea of having to take care of this thing was scary, and the actual work involved was the most painstaking of all of the responsibilities I was to ever have. It was going to be my job to change these end caps every day and to change the dressing at the chest site every five days. Because this line went directly into Ben's little heart, the tiniest of germs that came anywhere near my cleaning care could be life threatening.

A nurse spent nearly an hour teaching me the steps necessary to care for the line. In addition, I watched closely every time any nurse came into the hospital room to care for Ben and the hose, and I asked endless questions. They were all wonderfully patient with me and often offered words of praise for my understanding of my new responsibilities. Ben's surgery recovery took about six days. When we were discharged, the care of the hose was all up to me.

The process of taking care of our "garden hose" and its end caps took about twenty-five minutes each morning. The process of actually changing the dressing took nearly forty-five minutes, and that occurred every five days. We had supplies delivered to our house once or sometimes twice a week, and in those medical supplies came everything we needed for our daily and weekly tasks. Included were several Central Line Dressing Change Kits. These kits were shallow plastic boxes about six inches square and three inches high, and they contained everything I needed to do my job of changing the bandage covering the tube's exit site from Ben's chest.

Changing the caps became routine, and we managed easily. The complete dressing change was much more stressful. Benjamin sat on Chuck's lap facing me and firmly held each of Chuck's hands. Every five days, the three of us were tense and almost neurotic about having to do the procedure. My hands shook as if I were a very elderly, frail, timid woman. Because Ben was terrified when he had to go through this dressing change, I tried to help him by establishing a routine, a methodology, and a very rigid pattern of doing this job so that he would somehow be less apprehensive. I figured that if he knew exactly what was coming and when, he would be able to deal with the fear and uncertainties more easily. Such a routine would hopefully reduce my anxieties, too.

Our very first step was to put on surgical masks that covered our noses and mouths. Anyone else in the room also had to wear a mask or, better yet, leave the room. We were usually alone as a family, but often Miss Patty or Grandma or a caring friend would be there. They all understood the importance and gravity of the procedure, and I was really grateful that they respected the time, space, and sterility necessary for this job. There was enough stress involved as it was, and there was no need to worry further about who was breathing in the room.

After everyone in the room had donned a mask, I would very gently tear back the paper top on the kit, not allowing any of the contents to spill out. I then used the contents of the kit to prepare a sterile field. First, I had to gently reach into the container and pull out the folded paper sheet. It was a job in itself to carefully open the twenty-four-inch square, white paper and lay it on the table without touching anything in the process. This sheet was the base of the sterile field. I first held the very edges of two corners and tried to shake it open. I was instructed to not shake too hard, however, or I would capture germs floating in the air and immediately contaminate my field base. It took a lot of practice, but I learned to open the sheet and spread it flat on the table in only a few seconds.

The next step was to don one of the sterile gloves. I usually fitted it onto my left hand while leaving my right hand free to work on organizing the rest of the supplies. Three sticks with alcohol swabs on the ends; three of the same kind of sticks with Betadine swabs on the ends; an antibiotic-soaked, penny-sized "donut"; and a six-inch, clear dressing top called a Tegaderm all had to be carefully opened and placed onto the flat, blue sheet without touching anything that would be considered a germ. At first it was almost impossible to arrange these supplies with the use of only my right hand. After several weeks of dressing changes, though, I have to admit that I became skilled with my dexterity, and my movements became much more precise and fluid.

When everything was ready on the sterile supply field, it was time to go to work on Ben. I had to continue to keep my left hand from

A Test of Faith

touching anything while I used my right hand to remove the dirty bandage from Ben's chest. This was always a tough job as he cried when the clear plastic sticky tape pulled on his skin.

"No! Don't do it!" he screamed. Chuck held our son's hands tightly. Ben kicked his feet at me and cried, "I said NO, Mommy!"

I tried to comfort him, but nothing ever helped. At times I found myself almost yelling at him. "Hold still, Benjamin. I have to do this!" Chuck also had to control himself from yelling at our innocently frightened boy.

I tried so hard to pull the tape off gently, and I tried so hard to go slowly, but it was still a tedious and painful process. I would become so nervous that my hands would shake. On other occasions, I found myself not taking any breaths underneath my mask or breathing heavily as if I had just run a race. If it was evening and I had already removed my contacts and put on my glasses, it was certain that my lenses would fog up. Chuck would have to reach up and remove my glasses for me. Ben always yelled when Chuck let go of his hands to help me to see more clearly. No matter how many times we told him that Daddy was just letting go for a second, it did not matter. Ben still yelled and panicked when he was not squeezing the blood out of Chuck's hands.

When the old dressing was free around all of the edges and was left attached only at the site of the hose exiting Ben's chest, I had to move as slowly and cautiously as possible. The sticky ball of the old dressing had to be pulled off even though it was often entangled around the hose. I had to use just the one ungloved hand to remove it while being extremely careful not to tug too hard, or I might pull the hose right out of his chest. That was the first thing the doctor and nurses taught me: "Do not let anything tug on this line, or it could pull right out of his heart." If that happened, the risks would be tremendous for severe bleeding and definitely infection, as air could potentially go right into the heart. No wonder my heart pounded when I reached this stage of the process.

"Don't pull out, please don't pull out," I repeated over and over to myself.

Finally, when I had safely removed all of the old dressing, it was time to begin the technique of a sterile cleaning process. I gloved up my right hand using the other sterile glove provided in the kit and then began. It never failed that I would forget something or develop an itch after I was sterile.

We started with the "brown soap," as we affectionately named the Betadine. Starting at the hose's entry site, I began to work, cleaning the skin on his chest in a circular motion out and away. I moved the swab in a slow circle until Ben's chest had about a silver dollar-sized brown spot on it.

"NEVER go towards the hole in his chest," said the nurse. "ALWAYS go from in to out." Her words played over and over again in my mind.

Brown soap number two, same procedure. Ben would scream, "No, Mommy!" I promised him that the brown soap would not hurt. Now number three, and we were done with that step. I had to remind myself to breathe.

The brown mess had to dry for about thirty seconds to be able to perform its germ-killing job. We all relaxed while we waited for it to dry. We tried to play a game where we would count to thirty out loud, but whenever we reached twenty, Ben would start to cry and squeeze Chuck's hands more forcefully, for he knew that next came the "white soap" that we all hated. Not only did the alcohol smell even through our masks, it also stung terribly on Ben's sensitive skin that was already pink and irritated from the removal of the old dressing.

We went through the same routine for the "white soap" with all three swabs, and I tried to work quickly but accurately. Every time Ben would cry and squeeze Chuck's hands so hard that his fingers turned white. Chuck grimaced but held on. Ben's cheeks would be wet with tears, and I was petrified that one of those tears was going to drip down onto his vulnerable chest.

The alcohol dried instantaneously, which was helpful because it allowed us to quickly move on to the next step. It was good to take the focus off the part that upset Ben so badly. After the alcohol cleaning, it was time to put the penny-sized, antibiotic-soaked gauze pad known as the "donut" around the hose where it came out of the chest. This pad was supposed to work prophylactically by keeping the hose site surrounded by germ-fighting medicines. If any bacteria dared to get close to try to creep into the hole in Ben's chest, this antibiotic-soaked donut pad would kill it and prevent it from doing any harm.

The small, quarter-inch thick disk of gauze was not a complete circle but had a cut through it. I was able to slip the open section around the hose to fit it into its proper position right up against Ben's chest. It worked very well and was pretty easy to handle. I was happy to have the donut in place with its germ-killing features. It gave me a reason to give a sigh of relief. The hole was covered, the site was less vulnerable, and we were almost finished.

In dealing with a three-year-old patient, it just seemed to make sense to give every procedure, instrument, machine, supply, or other medical necessity a common and relatively fun name. This practice always seemed to help Ben manage the events to come. By giving the procedure, medicine, or test a pleasant name, we seemed to cope with it a tad easier. Hence, "brown soap," "white soap," "red light-green light pictures," "donut," and so on. It worked. Not just for Ben, but for all of us.

The final stage to the dressing change was to cover everything up with the new, clear Tegaderm pad. The Tegaderm was like a thick Saran Wrap with a super sticky backside. The six-inch dressing was a nightmare to work with. As soon as I removed the adhesive backing, it would always get tangled up in itself, stick together, and end up as a wadded mess on the floor. After many unsuccessful tries with the large six-inch dressing, we finally decided to switch to a four-inch size bandage, which managed to work just fine. I especially liked using the smaller four-inch covering because there were two inches less of the pad to pull off, and less red, sore skin underneath when dressing change time came again. I never dreamed five days could go by so fast!

The caps at the end of the hoses were changed daily. Although the cap change was similar in its intensity to the dressing change, it was much quicker. A "brown soap" scrub with the little square three times was followed by a "white soap" scrub with a standard alcohol square three times. Then I twisted off the cap, had the new sterile cap ready to twist on, and we were nearly finished. The final step was to inject both saline and Heparin into the line. We called this a "flush," and it was done every day.

We had boxes and boxes of syringes in our supply case and many small vials of both the saline (sterile salt water) and Heparin (an anti-clotting drug). I would draw out, or fill, two syringes of the saline, each five cc's, and two of the Heparin, also five cc's. When the syringes were set, it was time to flush. A specific list of steps in my head gave me the security that I was doing everything correctly. First, I had to wipe the end of the cap with Betadine and then wipe with alcohol. Second, I stuck the blunt tip at the end of the saline-filled syringe into the cap's end, unhooked the clamp halfway up the line, and slowly pushed. If I pushed too fast, Ben would holler at me to slow down.

"Hey, that's cold, Mommy!" he'd yell.

I'd re-clamp, pull the tip of the syringe out, and we were done with the saline. Next came the Heparin and the same steps.

Ben did not mind the cap change at all. By the time we had completed our first week of cap changes, Ben was more interested in the cartoon on the television than what I was trying to do.

"Hey, you're in my way, Mom."

"Oops, sorry," I'd say as I smiled.

Gloves off. Masks off. And we were done. I looped the long hose around a couple of times and then taped it up near Ben's sternum so that there would be no chance it would catch in his trouser waistband.

As soon as we were finished, I always put both of my hands on Ben's cheeks, pulled him close, kissed him on the forehead, and said, "Great job, Bud!"

He would jump from Chuck's lap and run off to play as if there was nothing wrong, new, or different with his body. Chuck and I watched him nervously, both of us hoping that nothing would catch on that garden hose.

Normal little boy activities were modestly altered for our three-year-old. No rough play, no contact play, and, much to his pleasure, no normal baths, all because of the Hickman catheter. For the five-and-a-half months that the line was in place, Ben could sit in a very shallow tub of water, but from the waist up, he had to be carefully sponged clean. No water could pour down from his face or head because of the risk of it going directly to his chest. Keeping him clean was a tough program because Florida's heat can produce some dirty and smelly little armpits. I wonder if baldness resulting from chemotherapy in a kid with cancer was possibly a gift. Not having to wash and rinse a head full of hair made things a lot easier on me. I managed to give Ben his bath every night and had my boy clean from head to toe.

The responsibilities at this stage of the journey were incredibly intense, but we made it through. I am proud to say that Ben never had an infection in his central line, and, more importantly, we never had the line pull out.

By taking on these home nursing duties, I was finally filling many hollow spaces in my heart. There were so many times that I felt completely helpless during this journey that accepting the challenges of caring for Ben's central line actually helped me to cope. I was glad I could finally do something besides pray for my son.

13

Harvesting

Two-and-a-half weeks after surgery, Ben was looking fantastic. His cheeks were rosy for the first time in months, and he had an incredible sparkle in his eyes. My boy was back!

Chuck and I had been to Duke twice for interviews and tours within the past two months, but now it was time to take Ben. We made the trip to Duke University Medical Center with Benjamin and Dana in late April 2001, just three weeks after the surgery. The purpose of the trip was twofold: first and foremost, we had to have Ben's cells harvested for transplant, and second, we had to look around town to figure out where we were going to live when we returned in four weeks.

The harvesting procedure was an example of medical technology at its best. The entire procedure of harvesting, or collecting cells, was actually quite amazing. For several months prior to this trip to Duke, we were required to give Ben an injection every day of a Granulocyte Colony Stimulating Factor, or growth-stimulating hormone, called G-CSF. The man-made protein, also called Neupogen, was a stimulating formula that was used to move the stem cells out of the bone marrow and into the circulating bloodstream. By doing this, we were increasing our chances of a successful harvest. We needed as many stem cells in the bloodstream as possible so that they could be captured and saved for the eventual bone marrow transplant.

The injection each night was another stressful event for our family. The needle was very long and very thin, but, nonetheless, it was a needle, and children hate needles. We again tried the idea of having a routine, but when it came to getting (and giving) a shot, nothing was easy. Ben bared his little thigh, I swiped it with a small alcohol swab, and then, on the count of three, I stuck the needle in and pushed the contents of the syringe into his leg. He yelped as he experienced the burning sensation, gritted his teeth, and asked over and over again through his cries, "Are we done yet?"

I covered the small puncture wound with a cartoon Band-Aid. Each night, Ben was allowed to choose the bandage because I wanted to give him some control. After all, every minute of every day it seemed that someone was telling him what he had to do and what was going to be done to him. The least I could do for the kid was to let him select his own Band-Aid. We had a selection of Blue's Clues, Sesame Street, Winnie the Pooh, Toy Story, and Arthur. I never could guess which one he'd choose, so I laid out the entire selection on the kitchen table. It was a good game, all in all, because it made the twenty-minute procedure bearable: we ended on a good note. It was sort of funny, too, because if I ever cut my leg shaving during those months, the only choice of Band-Aid available to patch up my wound was one of those colorful, bold, bright adhesive tapes. Everyone at work would then tease me about my Band-Aid.

The harvesting procedure took place in a small room right on the transplant unit at Duke. The "space room" was located about two doors down from the parent room, right next to the doctor's sleeping quarters. To go to this procedure room, we had to walk in the hall of the transplant unit, which was good because we saw firsthand where Ben was going to be living for many, many weeks. Walking in the hall of the transplant unit was also very horrifying. I felt again as if I were watching a movie being played in very slow motion. Everyone and everything around me seemed to be hardly moving. The mood was extremely solemn and serious. I felt as if I were watching things from under water; everything and everyone was moving slowly and with great effort, and objects seemed completely out of focus.

I could hardly move my feet when we first arrived at the unit. It seemed as if I had concrete in my shoes, and it was nearly impossible to pick one foot up to move it forward to walk. The children all looked so sick. They could hardly stand upright and relied heavily on the support of parents holding onto their arms. Their eyes were dark and tired as they looked out over their masked faces. They were all bald and extremely pale. Some of the children actually looked gray. What seemed like miles of plastic tubing was tangled around the IV poles. Bags of fluids hanging from the poles looked heavy and cumbersome as they swayed back and forth on their hooks.

Sandie Klassen

The parents looked completely wiped out. Everyone was one hundred percent exhausted and looked as if they had not slept in weeks. Most of the parents were dressed in wrinkled sweats and easy slip-on shoes. Their hair was disheveled, and bags and dark rings framed their eyes. I tried to give them a weak smile as we passed, but I'm sure I could not hide my look of complete shock. I was paralyzed with fear, and I know now that each person I saw that morning knew it.

Having seen all of this, both Chuck and I grew more and more worried about going to bone marrow transplant. I could tell that this was going to be the most difficult time of my life, and I was sorry to say that I was really dreading the idea of having to do it. It was such a selfish thought, but I did not want to go through with this, and I did not want my son to have to do it, either.

The harvesting room was called the "space room" because it was painted with astronauts, stars, and a bright yellow sun. When the nurse turned off the lights, the stars on the ceiling glowed in the dark. The room was designed and decorated to halt any intimidating feelings in the youngsters, and it worked well for us. A 27-inch TV was mounted in the corner with a VCR attached to it. Ben chose to watch an episode of *Bob the Builder* during the time it took to harvest his cells in the little room. He sat in an oversized, ugly, green leather recliner, ate goldfish crackers, and sipped on apple juice while he patiently waited for the medical procedure to be completed and for us to tell him that we were done for the day. He seemed pretty relaxed once he realized that he was safe and that nothing was going to hurt him during this procedure.

The process of harvesting cells was very interesting. It involved a machine about the size of a washing machine. It had a glass top on it, and you could look inside to see a drum barrel spinning around. The drum spun so fast that you really couldn't see any differentiation between the objects inside it. On a washing machine, the panel with the control dials is usually on top and at the back of the housing, and it is about four inches tall or so. This machine, however, had a back panel that was about eighteen inches tall, and it had a complex computer with several knobs and buttons on it. Off to the side but still attached to the harvesting machine was an enclosed glass case for a standard-size blood bag. We had become very familiar with this kind of blood bag during all the transfusions into Ben's body over the past

A Test of Faith

several months. There were long plastic tubes coming off the machine, and these were attached to each end of Ben's two lines.

The computer was programmed to pull blood out of Ben from one hose and to run it through the sophisticated spinning drum to separate the cells into two groups. One group consisted of the stem cells, and the other was composed of all of the other normal cells in the blood. The stem cells were then run into the enclosed hanging bag while the remaining cells were pumped back into Ben through the other connected hose. We suddenly understood why the Hickman catheter was required to have two branches to it. The procedure was monotonous, and Ben had to sit very still, so we were thankful that all was completed on that first day in only two hours. We had to go back to that room three times, for a total of six hours of harvesting. It took that long to collect enough cells to be sure that we would have the proper amount for an effective transplant.

The three bags of cells were unimpressive. The technician let me hold the thick plastic bag containing the stem cells for just a few moments before she took it to a cooler. The plastic bag felt warm and very light. It was only about one-eighth full, and the fluid inside looked like normal dark red blood. This, of course, was not the case. The stem cells in those bags were Ben's chance for a healthy life and a cure for this cancer.

The cells in those bags were going to be spun down even further. They would then be microscopically examined for purity, studied for volume and quality, cleaned, and finally frozen. The procedure was called "cryopreserved," which meant that the cells would be frozen at temperatures between -80 and -196 degrees centigrade. They would be kept frozen, stored somewhere in a freezer at Duke University, until Ben's body was ready to receive them back.

The strain and stress of all of the G-CSF, Neupogen, shots over the previous months proved to be well worth the countless tears, deep breaths, and sweaty palms. The cries and the screams, the pleading and the pressures were now reason to rejoice because when it came to harvesting stem cells, what was supposed to take five to six hours per session was completed in just over two hours. Everyone was thrilled. The technician paged the doctor to tell him of the success, and the doctor couldn't believe it. This was great news. Chuck and I really did not know how to respond because we did not realize how good of a deal this was, so we went along with the program and high-fived each other and Ben. We punched closed fists into the air and cheered a "Hooray, Ben!" At the same time, we silently gave thanks to God for the successes we were witnessing. His plan was being revealed more and more. Things were going to be ok for our son.

Harvesting the cells in only two hours per session indicated that Ben's central line was of a perfect diameter for his body, and it showed that the line was capable of handling a great amount of fluid pressure. This was important for what would be required at transplant. In addition, it showed that everything we were doing thus far was working in Ben's body. The medicines, hormones, chemotherapy, and prayer—everything was coming together to get us ready for the transplant.

Blood is composed of many different types of cells, each having its own specific function. The study of blood cells is fascinating, and it would take years of research to sort out all of the details. It is again one of those things where there is more there than meets the eye. A drop of blood has enough going on in it that one could spend an entire lifetime studying it. Thank God that some people are out in the world doing just that!

In a normal healthy adult, about 100 billion red blood cells and 400 million white blood cells are produced every hour. Basically, these cells will go on to develop into mature red cells, white cells, or platelets. Most of these cells are produced in the bone marrow, but the spleen produces some, too. When they are first produced from the bone marrow, they are very primitive and are called "pluripotent cells," or stem cells. These stem cells can divide, reproduce, make perfect duplicates of themselves, and even turn into other types of stem cells.

I had to think about it this way: suppose that you had a group of 100 two-year-old children in a huge gymnasium. Here you have innocent, beautiful, immature little people. They are all organized in rows, and they sit comfortably and quietly. When the bell rings, each of the 100 children jump up from their tiny seats and go off in a direction that they choose. Some go down one hall and become chefs and mailmen. Another goes down a different hallway and becomes a doctor. One goes out the back door and later becomes a lawyer. Three others go through the front doors and end up as accountants, bankers, and fast-food restaurant drive-thru attendants. Some stay right in their seats and never become anything. Some of them die.

God has a plan for each of these children. I truly believe this. He will, of course, give them many choices in their lives, but His goal is to have them develop and mature into what His dream is for their lives. It is the same with these stem cells. Some will become hearty red blood cells, some will become leukocyte white blood cells, some will become monocytes, others are destined to become lymphocytes, and some become platelets or thrombocytes. Some are probably destined to stay seated on their chairs and never go anywhere. Some are meant to die and do nothing. So, from these basic, primitive, immature cells, an entire new blood cell system can be made, just as an entire new world can be created by the little children in the analogy above. Our bodies and our blood are incredible systems that could only have been developed by a master planner. It is a system that is so well designed, interconnected, and intentional that I believe it could only have come from God.

After three days and a total of just over six hours of collecting baby cells, we had three bags of stem cells that were going into a freezer at Duke. Ben's hoses were all set, and we were about ready for what would be the most grueling and dangerous medical procedure a cancer patient could go through—a bone marrow transplant.

Dr. Driscoll discharged us to go home after the collection of cells was completed. Wishing us well, he recommended that we enjoy the next four weeks of freedom because our summer was going to be anything but free. He shook our hands, patted Ben on the head, and said farewell for now, as we were scheduled to meet again at this same place in just one month.

We still needed a place to stay when we returned to Durham, North Carolina. The social worker had provided us with a folder of maps and lists of places to stay around the university. We looked near campus for a safe apartment where we could make a home for the next five months. We looked at places where students usually rented and considered additional complexes of apartments where professional people from the famous "Research Triangle" stayed. We looked at even more areas of housing where local professionals and ordinary families lived. We checked out the Ronald McDonald House and the local extended-stay hotels. We looked into the churches to see if any families had housing available for rent, and we read through the local newspaper for other living and rental opportunities. Every place had its advantages and disadvantages, and every place was very expensive. The Ronald McDonald House was the only truly affordable option, thanks to the millions of people who donate their change to the Ronald McDonald House program when they go through the drive-thru at the McDonald's restaurants. That money does work to make life easier for parents with sick children.

As we looked for a place to stay, we also had to consider the needs of the others who would be staying with us. We never hesitated when it came to the decision to bring Dana with us to Duke because we could not bear the thought of missing her over the coming long months. Just the thought of not seeing her for the summer was enough to kill me, so there essentially was no decision to be made. She was going to Duke with her family.

We were excited and relieved when Miss Patty offered to go to Duke with us. She said that she wanted to help in any way that she could and thought that being there to care for Dana was the best way she could help. She was so right. It is still amazing to me that she offered to pack up, leave her family behind, and go along to help us during the most trying times of our lives. She was going to have her thirteen-year-old daughter, Lisa, with her, but every other member of her family would stay in Florida while she sacrificed her summer for us. I truly believe God sent Miss Patty to us as an angel. She is most definitely our angel, even to this day.

We finally settled on an apartment about three miles from the medical center. It was in a complex that was mostly occupied by Duke staff and students. The complex offered furnished, two-bedroom apartments with two bathrooms. The grounds included a clubhouse, pool, and well-lit parking lots. The buildings were tucked into the Duke Forest, and seemed fairly well kept. Here, we thought, we would be safe and comfortable.

We sat with the woman in the apartment complex's office, exchanged phone numbers, and wrote down our plans. It felt really good to know where we would be living for the summer. The office manager was very helpful and attentive while she sat taking notes. Per the doctor's orders, we had many requests that would need to be completed in preparation for our arrival. We were not the usual college students coming in for a school-year lease; we were a family bringing our son to one of the top universities in the world to have a bone marrow transplant. Per the doctor's orders, we would need an apartment with new carpeting, new air-conditioning filters, and fresh,

A Test of Faith

clean bedspreads. We had to have a place where no pets had lived. Fortunately for us, the office manager understood the needs of a transplant family. She had previously had others like us stay in her complex, so she was more than accommodating, and we were more than thankful.

It was hard to imagine that the apartment we rented that day would be our summer home. Renting a place for the summer would have been fun if we were planning a visit as tourists, but I knew that our stay in Durham would be anything but a vacation.

14

One Last Dose

The last course of chemotherapy was our toughest of all. With the tumor now out and the stem cells collected, the doctors all agreed that one last course of chemotherapy was a good idea. It was a safety precaution and one last provision taken to be certain that Ben's body was truly rid of all cancer cells. The doctors' speculations were that if any cell, by any chance, got loose and became active during the tumor removal, this last bolt of chemical poison would find it, destroy it, and make Ben's body pure for transplant. This step was not part of our originally planned protocol for the neuroblastoma, but we agreed that the doctors had a valuable idea. It all seemed to make sense, so we went for it.

The last course took about five days. We were admitted into the hospital back in Florida on Monday afternoon, and the large syringe of Vincristine was pushed into Ben's accessed port about 6:00 in the evening. The next step was to hang the large yellow bag of Doxorubicin on the tall pole beside Ben's bed and allow it to drip into his body over the course of an hour.

The administration of the medicine was slow and uneventful for the most part. Ben's shiny head barely peeked out from under the white blanket on the hospital bed, and he was cuddled up to his big, yellow Pooh Bear. He looked peaceful for the moment with a slight smile on his face as he rested. I decided to get some rest, too, in the chair beside him.

It was about forty minutes into the dose when Ben woke up frantically searching and yelling for his bucket. "Yikes, bucket!" he screamed.

I jumped out of my seat with my heart pounding and scrambled to grab the bucket at the end of his bed before it was too late. "Got it, Ben. You're ok, buddy," I whispered.

A Test of Faith

He began to dry heave into the pink pail while I reached for the nurse's call button to ask for some medicine to settle him down. By this time he was sweating and crying.

"Please, Mommy, tell my tummy to stop doing flip flops," he said. "I don't like this feeling."

I wanted to help him, so I talked directly to his midsection. "Hey you, belly. Stop that right now! Leave my boy alone!" I tried and tried to make Ben think that I could actually make a difference by talking to his tummy as he had asked me to do.

The nurse hurried in with a properly dosed syringe of morphine and quickly attached it to the pump for automatic infusion. The morphine slowly moved into the tubing; I could see the fluid making its way toward Ben's heart. Unfortunately, nothing was helping yet, and the dry heaves showed no sign of stopping. Ben's face was flushed from the pressure of the vomiting and wrenching, and his eyes were swollen and moist. He looked so pitiful that I had to look up at the television, even though it was not turned on, to conceal the tears I was shedding for him.

Ben tried to be tough, but he began to cry softly after enduring nearly thirty minutes of this miserable state. He finally put his face into his hands and started crying, holding nothing back. Soon he was sobbing, and through it, I could hear him saying, "I just can't do it."

With that, I started to cry, too. I just wanted to stop all of this. We had been going through this same routine for nearly five months now, and enough was enough. I hated it. It wasn't fair, and I just wanted it to be over.

The nurse came back into the room shortly after the morphine finished going into Ben to check on us. She was upset to see that our situation had not improved at all and Ben and I were both crying. She came over to me and put her hand on my shoulder. I felt an instant warmth and compassion pass through her to me. I felt as if someone cared about us, and we were not alone in this dismal situation. When she placed her hand on my shoulder, she gave a firm squeeze, and the sensation that flooded my body was like that of stepping into a nice warm shower on a cold day. Her touch made me want to cry even harder because she brought so much tenderness to the situation.

The nurse left again to phone the doctor for an additional order of something to calm Ben's stomach. I hoped that the pharmacy had a magical way to stop this reaction, but I was doubtful because we had tried nearly everything over the months. Vomiting and dry heaves were just normal side effects of chemotherapy. We had to be stronger.

For five days, we endured Ben's terrible reaction to the chemotherapy. We were all tired, frustrated, aggravated, and melancholy. It just seemed as if things should be getting better by now. I was wondering why we had agreed to this last dose of chemotherapy in the first place; it wasn't in the protocol, and it turned out to be torture for Ben. I ultimately knew that we did what was right, but at that moment, nothing seemed to make any sense at all, and I wanted it over. I just wanted to go home and take my son with me.

Ben finally settled down. When he began to stabilize with his weight and showed improvements in his ability to eat and drink, we were all relieved. The doctor decided it would soon be safe for us to take Ben home, which meant that we were officially ending the chemotherapy part of the protocol. Chuck and I were pleased about the news of going home soon but almost too exhausted and deadened of any emotion to express our joy. Like robots or zombies, we were at a point where we were just going through the motions without any thought. Ben, too. He was too tired and too weak to stand, and he was literally debilitated. We had to dress him, carry him, and take care of all of his personal needs for him, but that was ok.

When I carried Ben, I was able to hug him tightly, and that was all I wanted to do. He could not hug back for his arms were too heavy and feeble to do anything. His worn eyes just gazed at us, and his washed-out face held absolutely no expression. It was so sad to see him that way. His suffering was too much to bear any longer. I wanted to go home and just sit with him in my arms. I wanted everything quiet, and I wanted to be alone with him. For the very first time since the diagnosis, I did not think it was worth the fight any more. I wanted to go away, far away. I wanted to go to heaven with Ben where we could both be renewed, strengthened, and free from all of this. I thought I was ready to give up. Enough was enough.

Two days later, we were discharged to go home. It always felt so good to remove the blue-checkered hospital pajamas and put Ben into his normal little boy clothes. He always looked so much healthier dressed in regular street clothes. We chose his favorite Everblades hockey T-shirt and green shorts. The green shorts were miserably ugly to me, but they were Ben's favorites. They were really an unsightly mix of lime green, forest green, and maybe some brown. Ben loved them, though, so that's what we brought for him. White socks and Nike gym shoes completed his outfit.

I packed the small duffle bag with our toothbrushes, sweatshirts, magazines, and slippers and waited for the nurse to come in to de-access Ben's port and sign the routine discharge papers. This was a normal process for us, and we were thankful that the discharge always went fast. We were ready to go home.

Chuck was pulling the car up to the front of the hospital along the horseshoe drive just as we made our way through the front door. I was sitting in the wheelchair, and Ben was resting on my lap. As soon as the nurse pushed us outside, I immediately noticed the incredible blue, Florida sky that never ceased to inspire me. The warm sunshine hit my face, and a feeling of exhilaration went through my soul. I hugged Ben tightly and felt a sudden passion for life again. Feeling Ben's little heart pounding beneath my hand, I instantly forgot about the struggles that we had endured over the week. I forgot about the vomiting and the pain and the loss of our will to fight. I suddenly wanted nothing more than life again and a beautiful future for this child.

I was embarrassed that just a few days earlier I was thinking about giving up. The hospital room and the chemotherapy had tried to defeat us, but the warm sun and blue sky brought us back. Breathing in the fresh air, I realized once again that life is beautiful, and it is a gift. It was our responsibility to take off the ribbon, unwrap the package, and dig in to experience and enjoy. This little boy had a whole world ahead of him to which he needed to say hello.

In that Florida sunshine, I felt alive again. I had intensity and desire within me that were bursting to get out. I was ready to fight with every bit of my heart and soul to save this boy and give him a chance at a future. I wanted him to be a grown man who was healthy, happy, and able to show this same sky to his children. I felt more determined and committed than ever to help him to do just that.

For a moment, the emotional roller coaster I was riding threatened to drive me crazy. I wondered how in the world I could go from one extreme attitude on life to the complete opposite, but I rode with it. I had to trust that I was not losing my emotional stability. I thanked God for the gift that he had just put back into my heart. I thanked the nurse, too, for all of her help. Then I stood up and stepped away from the wheelchair. I turned Ben around so that I was hugging him chest to chest, and I spun him around slowly and said, "Look, Ben, everything is going to be ok. Look at this sky, buddy. Jesus is taking care of us. You are the best, kiddo!"

He smiled at me and said something that I could not understand.

"What was that, Ben?" I asked.

"Mommy," he said more clearly and with a suspicious smile on his face, "you are crazy!"

"YES, I AM!" I shouted. "I am crazy about YOU, Ben!! Let's go home and see Dana."

Ben was soon buckled into his car seat, and we headed home. We did not have to return to the hospital clinic for two days. Two full days of freedom. Two days where we could be together laughing and playing and living. Two full days just to be a family together in our home. We were going to have time for the four of us to experience the magic, wonder, brilliance, and fascination of each other and our life together. We had two days left before we were leaving for Duke. We were going to beat cancer. We were going to win the battle, and we were going to celebrate with the rest of our lives.

15

Our Farewell

The two days at home seemed but a fleeing moment. The days passed swiftly as we played together, read together, watched a movie, and prepared for our trip. We packed six suitcases, three large soft-sided bags, and several boxes of things we would need while in North Carolina. Fortunately, our big Ford Expedition had enough cargo space to hold everything, but it was a tight squeeze. There was barely enough room for Chuck to fit into the driver's seat, so it was a good thing that the doctors had advised Ben, Dana, and me to fly.

Miss Patty was going to fly with us to help me with the children, so she had her car packed solid, too, with all of her summer clothes and personal belongings. I still could not believe she was doing this for us. Her daughter Lisa was going to fly up one week later when the school year ended, but Patty was ready to leave with us. I must have thanked her a thousand times for making the trip, and I still need to thank her a thousand more.

When I was a child, my parents always had me call adults by a title of courtesy followed by their surname. It was proper behavior and a sign of well-mannered children. It was also a sign of respect for the adult. I liked the custom. I decided to teach the same etiquette to my children because I thought it would instill in them the value of respect toward others.

We were overjoyed when Patty accepted our nanny position. She had three teenagers of her own, a very loving husband of twenty-five years, and one amazing gift from God. If you met Patty at the grocery store and started a conversation with her, by the time the few minutes of talk had ended, you would want to hug her before departing. Patty was that kind of person. Her effervescence was contagious and so was her kind, loving, and gentle spirit. We had looked long and hard for the perfect person to care for our children during the day. We waited and waited because we were very particular for obvious reasons.

Finally, we decided to pray about the person who might be interested in helping us with the most important job in the world, and along came "Miss Patty."

The plan for the trip to North Carolina was for Miss Patty to bring her packed car to our house very early in the morning. Our friend Rodney was going to meet us at the house then, too. Chuck was going to drive our vehicle, and Rodney was going to follow in Miss Patty's car. They were going to leave right before dawn so that they could spend the entire day on the road. The drive was approximately fifteen hours, which would include lots of bathroom stops for Chuck. He was worse than a potty-training toddler when traveling and had to make frequent pit stops. I giggled when I told Rodney what to expect. He didn't believe me, but he soon learned that I was not kidding.

Rodney was so nice to offer his time to help drive all of our stuff up to the university. In Durham, he would spend the night helping us to unpack and then fly back to Florida. It was going to be a very long twenty-four hours for him, but he willingly offered and basically begged us to let him help. We needed the help, and we were so thankful for his offer.

We had learned several months earlier that when you are a family battling cancer, you couldn't do it alone. You need to say "yes" to the neighbor who wants to bring you a hot meal. You have to let people help by mowing your lawn and running to the grocery store for you. There are so many things in the day that need to be done, and it is nearly impossible to do all of these chores and still care for your sick family member. The Bible says that you need to do unto others, as you would have them do unto you. If you are trying to help someone and they will not allow you to help them, then you cannot fulfill your duty as a Christian. That's why we accepted Rodney's offer to help.

At last we were as ready as we could be to go to Duke for the bone marrow transplant. I felt high-spirited and vivacious. I was ready to go north to make a difference in the world. I was ready to see Benjamin set records of recovery. I wanted to get out into the real world and show them what a family with faith could do. I was ready to conquer the mountain ahead of us, and we as a family were going to the summit with jubilance.

Miss Patty stayed with Dana while I took Ben to Dr. Salman's clinic that morning. We had one last visit there before our flight was to leave later that afternoon. I didn't think the visit to the doctor that

A Test of Faith

morning seemed necessary, but as always, I did exactly everything the doctor advised me to do.

Ben had his examination by Miss Debbie, his nurse, and then by Dr. Salman. We had a few minutes to wait while they both took important phone calls, so Ben and I went back to the patient snack area, a mini kitchen, to get a treat for him. He chose the individual size can of Pringles and a Pepsi. While he sat and ate his chips, I met with the doctor and Miss Debbie and received the heavy pack of films and reports that I was hand- delivering to Dr. Driscoll at Duke. The films were from each and every scan that Ben had had since day one. Every MRI, CT, Bone scan, X-Ray, MIBG film, and a copy of his thick medical chart were included. Probably a hundred copies of papers were in the envelope and more than forty-eight large films. I suddenly realized that I held every report written on Benjamin since that first Friday months ago. I stared at the packet in my arms and then looked up at Dr. Salman and Debbie. My eyes were teary as I thanked them. So many families never had a chance to go to transplant. They did not make it that far, but we did.

We had made our way to the waiting room and were about to leave the clinic when Sandy, the receptionist, called us back into the main hallway beside the front office. Sandy was perfect for her job. Many times, we walked into the clinic feeling somewhat weary and bored with the routine, and there would be Sandy sitting at her desk. You could never guess from visit to visit what color her hair would be. Once it was fluorescent orange, and the next trip it was bright green. Sometimes she would wear a pair of Groucho Marx glasses with big, black rims and an attached fake nose and mustache. She would grin behind her comical attire as she welcomed us with "Hello, Benjamin."

Ben always looked at her, gave a sheepish grin, and signaled with a body language nod of "What is she up to now?" He'd throw her one of those "whatever" waves and go right to the playroom. He always laughed at home about "goofy Sandy," so I know that he thoroughly enjoyed her antics. I did, too. She was just plain nuts, and we sure appreciated it.

On this day, Sandy called us back into the main hallway. As we entered the hall, there stood the entire staff, about fifteen of them, huddled together. They held up a huge banner that read, "Good Luck, Ben!" Each and every one of them had signed it. A portable tape recorder was on the windowsill, and someone pushed play. Ben just stared at all of them trying not to let the glowing smile underneath break through. The music began to play "Who Let the Dogs Out," Ben's all-time favorite hockey song. They sang together, completely off key, but they were cheering and raising their arms and having a blast.

By this time my cheeks were wet, and I was sobbing with joy. This crew had become family. They loved us and wanted us to win as much as we did. Dr. Salman hugged Ben with a great bear hug, and so did Miss Debbie. Ben still held his potato chip can and was grinning from ear to ear. It was the best thing they ever could have done for us on that departure day.

Ben and I sang and cheered as we drove back to our home. We played our song "Celebrate Jesus, Celebrate!" It was on my *Songs for Worship* CD, and we played it on each and every trip to and from the hospital. We would open all of the windows in the car, including the sunroof, to "go crazy." We'd play the music loudly, we'd sing even louder, and we'd wave our hands in the air and out the window and through the sunroof. The people at the stoplights must have been sure that we were totally insane, and we were.

We were going to Duke today. We were going to the home of the greatest of college basketball champions. They were winners, and so were we.

I yelled in the car, "Yes! We are the best, Ben, and we're going to DUKE! Thank you, Jesus!"

Ben replied, "Yeah, thank you, Jesus! We're going to DOOOOOOK!"

A Test of Faith

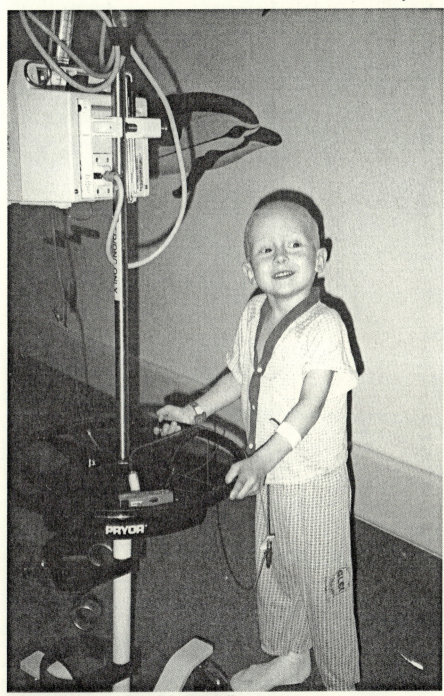

Ben getting used to his "pole".

Sandie Klassen

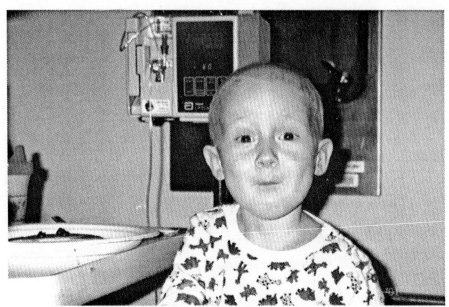

Dr. Salman's pancakes...Yummy!

A special blood drive. Electronic sign generously donated by a friend.

A Test of Faith

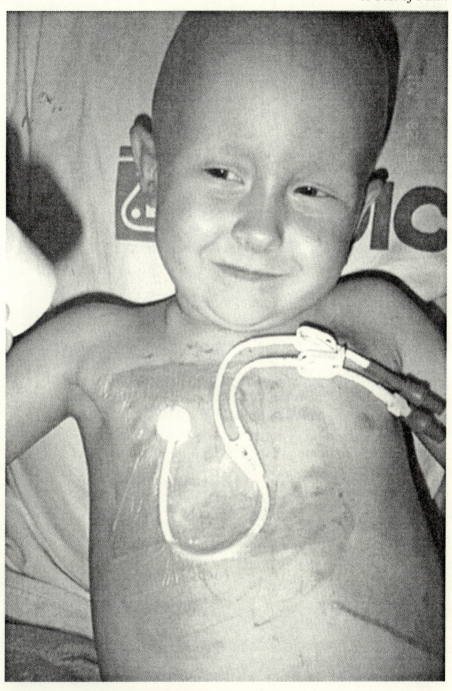

Our new "garden hose".

Sandie Klassen

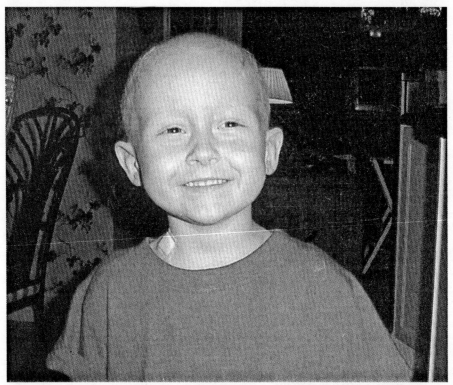

Finally home!!! Getting ready for DOOOOOOOOK!

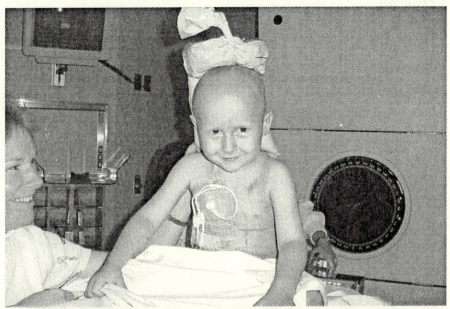
At Duke, preparing for radiation.

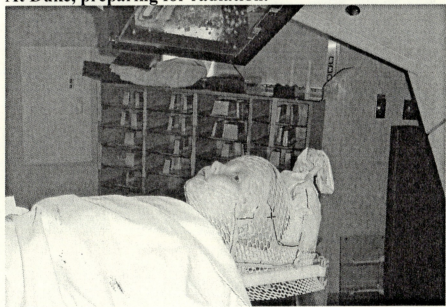
Radiation treatment.

Sandie Klassen

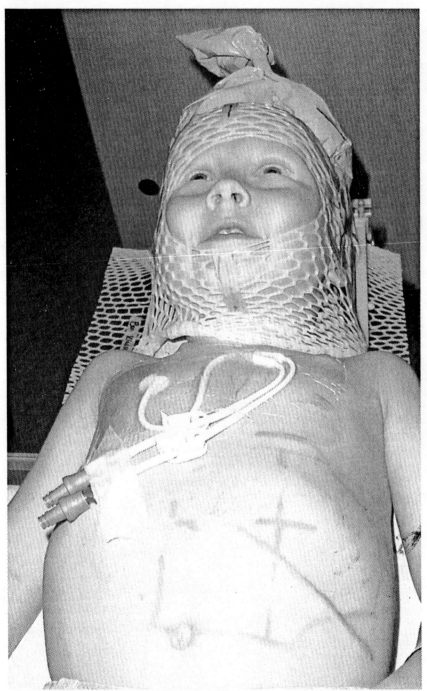

Our radiation "hockey mask".

A Test of Faith

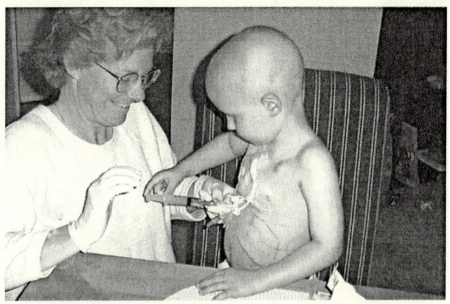

Flushing our hoses.

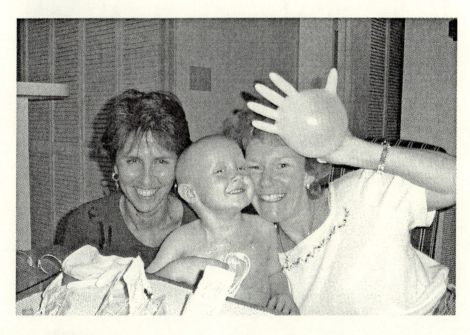

Having fun with Miss Patty while taking care of medical business.

Sandie Klassen

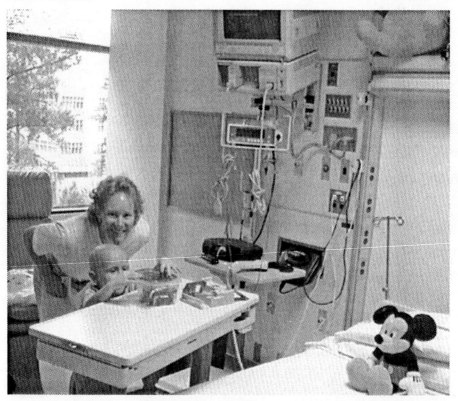

Mommy and Ben moving into our transplant room.

A Test of Faith

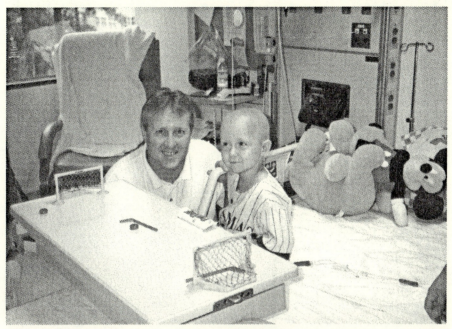

Daddy and Ben in our tiny room at Duke.

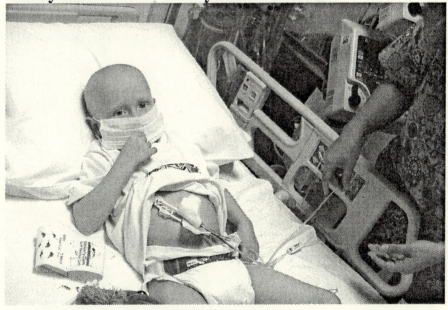

Preparing for our new cells.

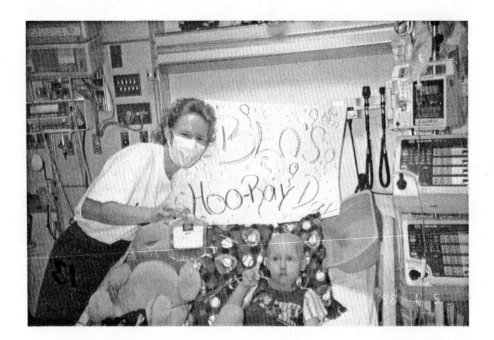

Transplant Day!!

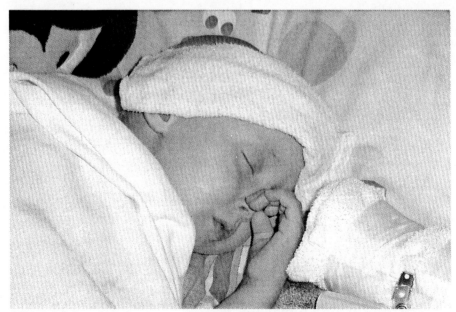

Mucositis and fever – A very sick boy.

A Test of Faith

Ben asleep in his bucket.

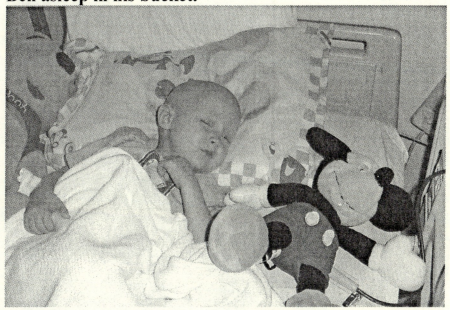

Grow cells Grow!

Sandie Klassen

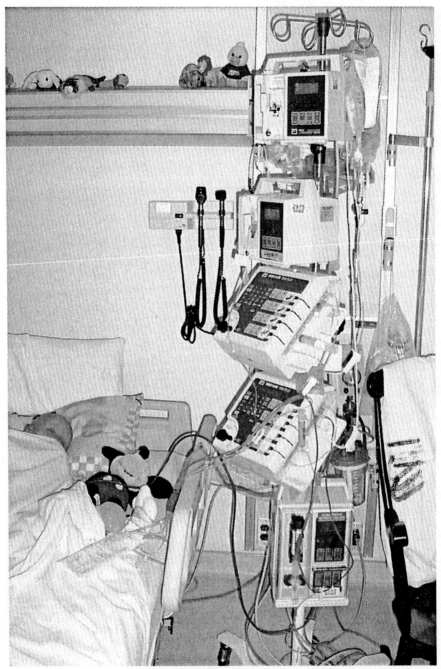

Pumps and more pumps for medicines and more medicines.

A Test of Faith

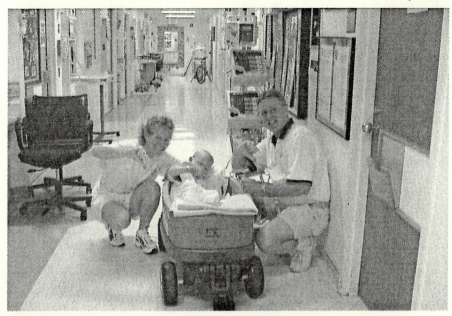

A thumbs down day for Ben. Mom and Dad happy he is finally up and moving.

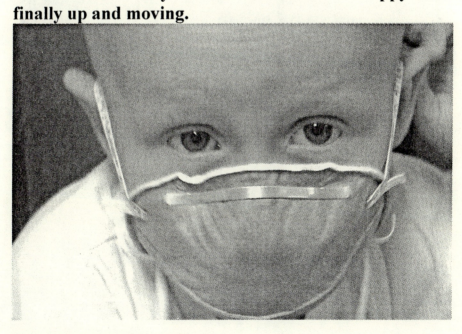

The green mask.

Sandie Klassen

Free at last and having fun with Dana.

A Test of Faith

One year later…Ben get splashed by Shamu at Sea World…Live for the moment!

16

Apartment Life

The last time I moved into an apartment, nearly twelve years ago, I was in graduate school. Then I was excited; today I was just plain nervous. Chuck and Rodney had not yet arrived in Durham, so Miss Patty watched Ben and Dana by the pool while I signed the lease in the office. I did not even read the stack of papers; I just signed my initials at the bottom corner of each page, scribbled my full name on the last page, and then wrote a check.

We had decided to drain our savings account if necessary because we were determined to take Ben to the best facility that medicine had to offer. In addition, we decided that we were going to do what we had to do financially to have a basic sense of security and comfort in our living arrangements during this time. We decided that with Miss Patty's commitment to go with us to help with Dana, and in any other way that she could, the least we could do for her was to get her an apartment of her own next door to ours. We knew that we would need time alone and privacy as a family, and we felt that she would, too. Everyone needs his or her personal space, especially when the stress level is high.

So, I wrote the check to the apartment complex to cover the first month's rent on the two apartments. The check was for $3200! The cost for one month's rent on two completely furnished apartments was outrageous, but this was the average price for any of the apartments near campus. They had you in a crunch because if you wanted convenience, you were going to pay for it.

When Ben was first diagnosed, the Rotary Club of Bonita Springs, Florida, Noon Club, came to our office and gave us a check for $500. I could not believe the generosity of this local business professionals' organization. I was so touched that I did not know what to say but "thank you." Those two words, however, did not seem sufficient, even though they were as sincere as they could be. I wanted to somehow express more deeply what was in my heart. I've learned

A Test of Faith

since that saying "thank you" with genuine sincerity is enough for most people if you really mean it, but it still does not seem to be enough for me. I wanted to say more. I wanted these people to see how full of gratitude my heart really was and how indescribably grateful I was for not just their money, but, more importantly, their love and concern for us.

Through this cancer, I have learned what it means to really care about others, support one another, and sacrifice for one another as the Bible says we should. After that first check and get well wish, hundreds more started to pour in. We received a total of 839 get well cards that ranged from folks we knew well to others whom we had not yet met and probably never will.

People sent money, stickers, happy faces, scriptures, bookmarks, ribbons, and a ton of love. Our mail lady smiled as she delivered the well wishes to our home from her old, white jeep. On several occasions, she brought the bundle of mail to our front door because there was too much to fit into our mailbox. One day, she put her own card into the bundle, too.

A fellow in our church started a Web site for us so that we could keep updates on Ben circulating through the community. At first, I did not think anyone would be interested in Ben's condition or the trials that we were going through because we were strangers to most of these people. I was wrong. Over 9000 people have since logged onto the Web site from all over the world! We had letters of hope and words of inspiration written from Michigan to Wyoming to Scotland to the North Pole. Ben was especially excited when we read him the note from Santa's hometown.

Two special ladies from our church organized a benefit dinner for Ben that included a silent auction and a sit-down, white linen dinner for seventy-five guests. People from the church and towns far away came to the event for Ben and our family. These two ladies had so many helpers for the dinner that I'm not even sure who was involved. The tickets sold out immediately after the announcement of the event, and an exorbitant amount of money was raised for Ben's medical bills.

The community we live in raised more money, and a loving friend gave an unbelievable monetary gift, too. All of these gifts were given with love in order to help us with our housing and additional bills while we were at Duke, and they prevented us from being totally devastated financially by Ben's diagnosis and treatment. Neighbors brought us dinner, someone cleaned our house, and family, friends, and strangers offered their time and even blood.

A blood drive was organized by a friend who did not know what else to do to help. She posted fliers all over town about the blood drive and the need for donations to help Ben. She organized food and refreshments from the local grocery store and received donations of other goods to make the event a first-class experience for all who were involved. An eight-foot-by-eight-foot electronic sign was even donated and placed on a busy highway announcing the time, place, and purpose of the drive. Ben's picture was programmed into the computer, and as commuters drove by, they could see exactly to whom their blood would be going.

On the day of the blood drive, hundreds of people began to pour in by 7:00 a.m. and continued to come until nearly 6:00 p.m. They had their shirt sleeves rolled up and were ready to give the gift of life. Ben was requiring so much blood during the course of his treatments that on occasion, we had to wait until the hospital received a transfer from another facility before Ben could get what he needed. It was expected that he would need at least fifty and up to one hundred more units during the course of his bone marrow transplant. With so many of the other cancer children needing similar amounts of the precious product, the blood bank was always in great demand for something that man has not yet been able to reproduce in a laboratory. The only way a patient can get life-saving blood products—such as red cells, platelets, or plasma—is from the donation of another person. Blood donors are the epitome of generosity: they give another person a renewed chance at life.

The drive that my friend organized and implemented turned out to be the largest ever in the history of our area with an unimaginable total count of 800 units of blood. A talented writer from the local newspaper called to do a story about the incredible turnout and altruism of the people who donated. She wrote a terrific article about Ben and our family, the hospital, the church, the blood drive, and the hope that we had. The story landed on the front page of the paper, accompanied by a large color photo of Ben, Dana, and me at a hockey game. Ben, dressed in his oversized Everblades jersey, was laughing and clapping as he watched his favorite mascot come out onto the ice.

A Test of Faith

The writer followed up with many stories about us to keep people informed along the path of our recovery. She told me later that each day after a story had been printed, her mailbox, voicemail, and e-mail were flooded with questions, compliments, and inquiries about how people could help. One of her stories on Ben reached a state journalist's contest and won her first prize and outstanding recognition for her expert work covering and presenting this human-interest story. Because of her articles and coverage of Ben, untold thousands of people suddenly became involved in this cancer story. Later, I learned that many of these people prayed for our success.

All of this benevolence and sincere unselfishness still astonishes me and brings me to my knees with amazement and appreciation. We were nobodies; we were just the people who lived down the street. We were just doing our normal thing—going to work, working hard, and raising our children. We were just trying to be the best people we could be, and we were trying to do what was right. People still reached out to us to offer their help when our son was diagnosed with cancer and was given a very slim chance for survival. People proved that the world is still very good.

Strangers often give me a very curious look when I say hello to them or strike up a brief conversation about the weather, the day, or whatever else comes to mind. I am proud to say that I do talk to strangers on a regular basis, and I am trying to teach Ben and Dana also to be socially healthy. It is part of my job to make people feel instantly welcome and at home in our business, and the great satisfaction I get from my work and these relationships carries over to my personal life, too.

I love to remember names and specifics about people; it comes naturally and is very easy for me because I really am interested in them. Ben liked the challenge I gave him to remember each and every nurse's name and her favorite color. When a nurse walked into our room, he would greet her by name: "Hi, Laurie," "Hi, Donna," "Hi, Kim." I was so proud of him. I truly think he came to enjoy their reactions, and he loved to see their surprised expressions.

On any day, if I come across someone who looks sad, mad, or indifferent, I make it a personal challenge to get them to smile before they are finished working with me. Ben loves this challenge, too, but as we have both learned, sometimes this is not easy to do.

Ben and I went to McDonald's for lunch one day and ordered our meals from a very indifferent employee. She wasn't interested in making eye contact, conversation, or anything for that matter. She became a great challenge to me. I had to go to McDonald's four times before I had a breakthrough. Finally, on that fourth visit, she gave me a curious but half-hearted smile. I persisted. By my seventh visit, I actually had her smiling and laughing. She told me that she had been behind that register for twelve-and-a-half years. I commended her on her loyalty and gave her compliments on how well she always handled my order. I grinned when I overheard her speaking to the next customer in line as I filled my Diet Coke at the beverage station. She was smiling and actually sounded enthusiastic.

Unfortunately, I grew incredibly tired of lunch at McDonald's and did not return for several weeks. When Ben and I again came in to order, we waited in this particular employee's long line. When it was our turn, I greeted her by name, smiled, and began my order. She remembered me! She said hello to me first, and then said, "Hi, Ben." She asked how our day was going and even said, "Where have you been for so long?"

My heart raced with joy and satisfaction over the little event. I was so gratified and enjoyed my McDonald's lunch with Ben more than I ever had before.

When people pull together, even the worst of situations can be turned around to the positive. Nothing can beat people who love each other, trust each other, and draw on faith to enjoy the lives they are given.

Our community pulled together for us and took us under their wing as family. We worked in incredibly vast numbers and rose up together to beat the cancer in Ben. We were not going to sit back and allow the tumor to destroy a young boy. Instead, we were going to fight as one, conquer, and prevail. We were going to be victorious for Ben's sake.

With all of the donations received in hundreds of cards, we opened a checking account at a local bank and named it "Ben's Medical Fund." It was from that account that I wrote the first rent check to the apartment complex on the day we arrived in Durham for the transplant. With all the things we had on our minds about taking Ben to transplant, we were so blessed not to have to worry about how

A Test of Faith

to pay for a place to live. Freedom from worry about finances was only possible because of what so many others did for us—they cared.

The manager issued me four keys, two for each apartment, and gave me copies of our lease along with a map to our units. Miss Patty, Dana, Ben, and I walked to the downstairs corner apartment first and opened the door. The outside of the door was filthy. It had so much dirt on it that it was like one of those vans that you often see driving down the road with "wash me" drawn in the dirt on the back window. Inside our apartment, there was a smell of both old cleaning chemicals and stale air. I looked at Patty, who must have been thinking the same thing: "What in the world are we in for?"

It only took us about a minute to walk through two bedrooms, two bathrooms, a small kitchen, and the single hall closet that housed the washer and dryer. We then sat on the couch and stared blankly ahead at nothing.

"We'll be fine, Sandie," Miss Patty said. "When the guys get here, we'll find a store and buy some cleaning supplies, and then we'll get it fresh and clean like home. Don't worry, we'll be ok."

Just then, a cockroach ran across the living room floor. I could do nothing but put my face into my hands and, guess what, cry.

Patty's place was located in the same building but not next door as promised. She was around two corners and up on the second floor at the far end. Her apartment was much cleaner than ours and even had evidence of some new paint on the walls. It wasn't without a few problems. The wallpaper in the kitchen was falling off, so we added tape and glue to our grocery list for some patch and repair work.

Chuck and Rodney arrived within the hour. We unloaded both of the vehicles into the appropriate apartments, and then we all sat on the couch in our apartment. We looked at each other and started sharing stories of all the places where we had slept over the years. A twenty-dollar hotel in Orlando once to conserve our money for Disney World (the shower there had mold an inch thick), a house with the door three inches off the ground in Japan when Patty's husband was in the military (mice and anything else made themselves welcome day and night), a park bench that my friend and I shared once in Europe when we could not find an available youth hostel, and more. We all ended up just laughing. It was so healthy and fun that all of a sudden everything seemed ok. Life was good once more, and we were going to be fine.

Sandie Klassen

That day in Durham, I again felt as if I was on an emotional roller coaster at an unfamiliar theme park. The coaster was taking me upside down a hundred times and was working at a G-force of almost five. It leveled out, slowed down, and then did its thing all over again. I was high and low, right side up and upside down. All I could do was laugh when I could and hang on for the rest of the ride.

The apartment looked a lot better after we took it through the deepest cleaning I am sure it ever had. We scrubbed until the sponges were falling apart and every bottle of bleach was gone. We washed the windows, blinds, floorboards, and the floors themselves. We scrubbed all over that front door and had the spider webs cleared from the entry area and the screened eight-foot-by-eight-foot porch. We even washed the bedspreads, just in case they were not cleaned as promised. We dusted on top of the lonely picture above the couch, and we wiped down the inside and outside of each of the five cabinets in the mini kitchen. We felt great when all was completed and felt safe to go to sleep in our new home away from home.

The office manager promised to arrange for the services of an exterminator for the next day. She said that the carpets were cleaned prior to our arrival, but we weren't so sure of that. The stains and heavy traffic areas looked otherwise, and I certainly was not going to let Dana crawl around on the disgusting carpet. I was reluctant to allow Ben to even walk in the apartment without wearing his shoes. Those poor children must have thought that their mom had gone off the deep end—I was way too compulsive. The office manager did agree, though, that the place looked terrible, and she apologized, and then promised that along with the exterminator, she would have the carpets attended to as soon as possible. I hoped I could wait that long.

The six of us were starving by late evening, so we found an old, tattered phonebook in one of the kitchen drawers and ordered from the first place that would deliver to the apartment. We ended up with Chinese food that was delicious. Ben and Dana ate most of the pork-fried rice, while we adults devoured the sweet and sour chicken, Kung po chicken, lo mein, steamed broccoli, egg rolls, and hot and sour soup. We had enough food to probably feed everyone in the entire apartment complex, yet the six of us ate almost every bite of it.

By the time we finished eating, our eyelids were very heavy as if we'd had a complete Thanksgiving dinner, so we situated ourselves for our first night in Durham.

A Test of Faith

Before I went to sleep, I got down on my knees (after, of course, putting a hand towel from the bathroom down on the floor), and I said prayers of thanksgiving for our safe travel and for our apartment. Mostly, I thanked God for the gift of love and support from our friends, family and God Himself. The only important thing in the world right now was that the good guy cells were winning. We were finally at Duke, and we had just one last punch to throw to knock out the bad guy cells forever.

17

Our First Day at Duke

It was 8:30 in the morning when Chuck, Benjamin, and I arrived in the colorful lobby of the Children's Hospital at Duke University. Twenty feet above us were giant circles of suspended orange, yellow, and red feathers. The feathers were arranged side by side and formed circles eight, nine, and ten feet in diameter. There were twenty-one of these circles in all: three yellow, eight red, and ten orange. Separated into groups of three or four, they looked as if they were free floating as they hung from the ceiling on clear filament fishing line. The 2,500-gallon aquarium was full of life as the tropical fish congregated near the man dropping flakes into the tank from his tall ladder. On the top of either end of the tank was an oversized stuffed animal: one was Sebastian, the red lobster from *The Little Mermaid* movie, and the other was a green and brown giant sea turtle. From the middle of the circular reception desk, a woman smiled as she greeted a family. A two-foot tall Elmo sat on the desk behind her.

The baby grand player piano was finished in richly polished ebony, and the sounds of the electronically produced music were equally as perfected and lavish. The programmed computer disc produced the tune of "Hotel California," and the keys of the piano worked as if someone were actually playing the beautiful musical instrument. It had been a long time since I had heard the melody from the old Eagles song, and it took me a moment to recognize it. I was quite certain that most of the patrons in the lobby had never heard it before. Besides the parents, the lobby was full of children with an average age of about six years. The children all bounced around happily, which amazed me because they appeared to be seriously ill. Most of them were bald or towed an oxygen tank on a small cart behind them or had tubes coming out of their noses. One sat in a sophisticated motorized wheelchair and had several braces supporting each of his extremities. He could not have been more than five years old, yet he was completely independent in moving the wheelchair around with the joystick in his right hand. A small girl, snuggled in blankets, sat in a plastic, green wagon. She grinned at the clown painting a flower onto her little, exposed leg.

The bright pink, grass green, and ocean blue glass elevators moved up and down on their visible gears and chains. They were full of people looking out into the cheerful, busy lobby.

"Wow, look at that elevator, Daddy," Ben said.

Across from the elevators was a massive wall, five stories in height, of plate glass windows. You could look through the windows out onto a playground for the children, which was complete with a fountain and a miniature "Coach K" basketball court. Beyond the playground was a busy scene of cars, buses, trucks, and pedestrians moving outside the hospital's front entrance.

Nearly every other person wore a white lab coat featuring pockets stuffed with papers, stethoscopes, and other doctor paraphernalia. Each had a Duke University nametag clipped to the collar, and I was amazed to see all of the "M.D." and "M.D., Ph.D." titles. These people had committed a significant amount of their lives to medicine. They were inspiring to me.

I glanced over at Ben, who had obviously lost interest in the elevators and was now profoundly occupied by the Thomas the Tank Engine train table. He looked carefree, content, and nearly spellbound as he parked each train car into the yard in the center of the tracks. Chuck and I sat in unblemished, dark blue cushioned chairs beside him and waited while he played for a few minutes. We were both glad that we had come to the clinic a bit early so that we did not have to rush up to the fourth floor where we would receive our very busy schedule for the day.

Our appointments were to begin at 10:30 that morning and would continue for the next five days. This was the pre-transplant workup that would be the most comprehensive study on Ben's body that had ever been done. He was scheduled for a pulmonary function test of his lungs, an echocardiogram of his heart, regular cat scans, spiral cat scans, scans with contrast, and some without. He had to have another MRI and a bone scan. A skeletal survey was on the list, too.

The MIBG was a special test scheduled for Ben. It was a very long nuclear medicine study that involved a sensitive and expensive isotope that would be injected into Ben via his central line. This injection would be followed by a series of radiographic pictures of Ben's body. The isotope was going to be delivered by Federal Express from Canada for the test because Canada was the only place where the highly sensitive radioactive material was manufactured.

We would have to do some protective preparation before we could begin the study, which meant that we had to give Ben a drop of a special medicine called SSKI in some juice for five consecutive days in order to protect his thyroid gland from severe damage. The radioactive material used for the scan would instantly destroy his thyroid gland if we did not first build an iodine shield around the sensitive structure.

Twenty-four hours after the first drop of the SSKI thyroid protector was ingested, Ben would be required to lie perfectly still for a three-hour scan of every cell of his body. The isotope was so well designed that it would attach itself to even one cell that showed cancerous activity. Active cancer cells release a certain enzyme that attracts this isotope. When it bonds to the receptor of a cancerous cell, it lights up the cell so that it can be seen on the nuclear medicine image. The actual picture looks like a traditional x-ray film.

We recognized that the MIBG scan was an example of the most advanced techniques in the industry, and we were glad to be able to benefit from the technology. We felt that we had been receiving excellent, quality medicine all along, and now, at this university that we had researched so intensely, we were going to experience every bit of the reputation that Duke had worked so hard to attain. As we looked at our list of appointments, we took note of a kidney function test, urine workups, full blood studies (twenty-seven different tests), sinus studies, a chest x-ray, and some meetings. Ben had to meet with the radiation oncologist and his group, the bone marrow transplant attending physician (Dr. Driscoll himself), the insurance coordinator, and the child life specialist. We had a very busy week ahead of us.

It was time to put on the running shoes and eat a hearty breakfast. We were off to the races.

18

Radiation

As part of the neuroblastoma protocol, Ben was to have fourteen doses of radiation to his head and abdomen, the sites of the removed tumor and spread of the disease. We were scheduled to meet with a radiation oncologist immediately after lunch. Although we were nervous, we were very excited to start this phase of our treatment.

We rushed through lunch, not able to finish our meal of turkey sandwiches, chips, and Diet Coke because we did not want to be late for our appointment. I was still chewing my last bite as we left the short-order restaurant on campus. Ben held a long, skinny, dill pickle in his right hand and bit off small pieces as he hurried along beside us to Duke's radiation department. We arrived at exactly 1:00 p.m. and were relieved to have not been a minute late.

The department was located in an industrial section of the medical center. Outside the front door, two smoke stacks from the power plant rose high above the trees like teenage boys standing among a crowd of kindergartners. My heart raced as I tried to settle into the waiting room chair. The furniture and wallpaper were old and worn but somehow fit the idea of "radiation." I felt as if I were in a bomb shelter. The waiting room was uncomfortably small with the walls butting right up to the sides and backs of the dozen chairs present. The ceiling was low, and the fluorescent lighting was very dim. There were no windows anywhere.

After nearly an hour, Chuck and I were beginning to feel aggravated and antsy, but we were still hopeful that our wait was going to be worth our time. We had heard extremely impressive details about the quality and skill of Duke's radiation team, and we were encouraged to have the opportunity to be there; that is, if we were ever going to be seen.

Our first glimpse of hope that our wait was almost over came when we were moved from the community waiting area to an exam room where we continued to wait. Ben played quietly with a plastic fire truck that was missing its windshield and one wheel. When the door to our undersized exam room finally opened, there stood a young woman who looked no more than twenty years old. She was dressed in a nice sweater and slacks and wore comfortable-looking laced shoes. She had a plastic tag hanging from her belt loop that revealed her name, followed by the letters "M.D." I had to look twice at the nametag to see that she was, in fact, a doctor. She shook our hands and then immediately knelt down onto the cold tile floor to greet Ben eye to eye. Besides Dr. Salman, I'd never seen any doctor do this, and I liked it. Within seconds, she had Ben laughing and playing and completely relaxed. She was a natural with the boy.

After nearly fifteen minutes of playful visiting with us, she said that it was time to begin. Her frolicsome ways began to fade like the end of a song, and the seriousness of our visit surfaced.

The doctor directed her attention to the matter at hand and began asking a few very frank questions to clarify her understanding of Ben's case. Although she did not look old enough to have completed high school, I soon realized that this doctor was nothing less than a genius. She was incredibly focused on the task at hand. She had obviously already studied every paper and report available on Ben because she knew dates, timeframes, and our history almost as well as we did. It was as if she had been with us all along, as if she were Dr. Salman. She knew Ben on paper only, however, and it was time for a real-life examination of the patient. When she stood up from her stool, she towered over both Chuck and me, who were still sitting. I suddenly felt the urge to stand, too. Somehow I felt that I was going to be better able to observe her examination of my son if I were on my feet.

The doctor studied Ben from every angle. She had our son lie down on a cold, leather-covered examination table, and then she slowly moved her fingers over and around Ben's bald head. Her touch looked delicate; it was as if the woman were handling the finest piece of china that she had ever seen. She studied Ben's tummy and again ran her fingers over his abdomen and rib cage. She traced her long, thin index finger along Ben's well-healed incision site, and then she stood back and held her right fingertip up to her lips while keeping her left arm folded across her chest.

A Test of Faith

The room was silent as she walked from one side of the table to the other and then back again, not once removing her eyes from Ben's little body. Finally, she helped Ben return to a seated position, patted him lovingly on his back, and kissed the top of his head. Then she sat back down on the scooter by the door.

She spoke formally using medical terminology, but at the same time, she picked Ben up and placed him on her lap. She spoke in a language of advanced medicine that was predominantly physics based, and it was accelerated physics at that. I scrambled to interpret and decipher the words presented, but it was much more advanced than I could remember from my years in high school and college together. Her language was very foreign even to me, and I had a significant amount of medical training. She spoke of electron beams, angles, refractions, protons and photons, fractionated and hyperfractionated administration, and densities of energy. Her mix of medical and nuclear physics terms made little sense to me.

She repeatedly used the word "irradiation" rather than simple "radiation," so I asked her what the difference was. She answered our questions as she stroked Ben's shiny head with her fingertips. He sat comfortably on her lap, enjoying her caresses.

She said that "irradiation" and "radiation" are two different terms by definition but that essentially, for all general purposes, they can be used interchangeably. "Irradiation" is the more accurate term when referring to the cancer-treating procedure.

I listened as attentively as I could, but I mostly sat stunned by this woman's brilliance. Her understanding of what needed to be done and to what degree seemed clear. She was certain that any chance of recurrence of cancer at the sites she was going to radiate was gone. Although she again became very playful with Ben and her intensely serious demeanor disappeared, she remained extremely confident in her abilities.

She concluded by shaking Chuck's hand and mine and once again dropped onto her knees on the floor. This time she embraced Ben with a bear hug. As she smiled widely at him and then at us, she suddenly looked more like a close friend or sister than the specialized doctor she was. The air in the room was as light as that of a fresh spring day. The doctor was remarkably intelligent, and she was human, too. She told us that she would study her notes again that night, and we could meet in two days for the preparatory work for the actual radiation administration. Wishing us a great day, she smiled and waved at Ben as she walked out of the room.

Although the meeting was nothing like I had expected, the radiation oncology meeting was extremely impressive. It proved to me that medicine does not have to be just business; it can still be old-fashioned caring.

The simulation for the radiation treatments took about three hours, but it only took Ben about three minutes to have the four technicians in the palm of his hand. The three hours flew by like a fun day at the park. The feeling in the room the entire afternoon, although serious with concentration, was also fun and very happy. Ben told his stories with every bit of detail he could muster up. He talked about the Florida Everblades hockey team; their mascot, Swampee (who is an alligator); his little sister and what she always does to him; and every other "You know what?" that he could come up with. It was as if he had known them for years.

I was filled with pride as I watched and listened to my baby talk so comfortably with these strangers in white lab coats. He was so confident, so social, so alive, and so loving. He was also so cute! I was in the palm of his hand, too. I couldn't figure how someone could ever love something more than I loved my child.

On and off throughout the simulation procedure, Ben had to hold perfectly still. The room was like many we had been in before with a huge metal piece of machinery, institution-like chairs, laundry baskets, x-ray light boxes on the wall, a leaded window off to the side, and bright lights. Ben was so brave as they worked to prepare his body for the radiation that would begin the next day. Dressed only in his Toy Story underwear, he lay on his back on the long metal table. The table was raised to a level that was just above waist height for the technicians so that they could comfortably work together taking measurements and checking positions. They looked over at x-ray films hanging on the lit box and noted the markings that had been made with protractors and delicate measuring instruments. They worked with the lights on for a while and then worked with the lights off. During the times the room was dark, a red laser beam shone onto Ben's face and forehead and then onto each of his temples and his abdomen. Each time the lights were turned on again, the girls continued to work diligently and with great concentration making purple marks on Ben's body and head. They drew all over his side and tummy, which made Ben giggle often.

The next step in preparing Ben for the morning's first dose of radiation was to create a plastic mask that would fit perfectly over his face. This mask would be secured to the table with large plastic clips during the actual treatments. Its purpose was to prevent Ben from being able to move his head even a fraction of a millimeter. If he did, the radiation would be directed to the wrong spot, and if it went to the wrong spot, it would damage normal, healthy tissue. The beams had to be one hundred percent perfectly directed, and there was absolutely no margin for error.

To help Ben better manage the difficult process of fabricating the tightly fitted mask, we decided to imagine that they were making him a custom-fitted hockey mask. The idea was perfect, and we all loved it, especially Ben, who allowed the technicians to work without conflict.

We watched as one of the girls took a large, thick sheet of plastic out of a box and made some drawings on it. She placed the plastic sheet that was filled with open spaces resembling a small chain link fence into a tray of boiling water. After the plastic softened, she and her assistant carefully held each of the corners and lifted the piece out from the tray of water. They carefully placed it directly onto Ben's face. They assured us that it would not burn him although it would feel warm. I still had doubts because as the plastic was lifted out of the boiling tray of water, I could see it steaming as if it were very, very hot. I was nervous as they stretched the flexible sheet of material across Ben's forehead, over the bridge of his nose, out towards his ears, and over his chin. As they smoothed it to his skin with their fingertips, a third assistant stood at the head of the table holding Ben perfectly still.

The radiation oncologist came into the room to check the markings and the progress being made on Ben thus far. Shortly thereafter, another radiation oncologist came into the room and gave her approval after studying the marks and mask. Both doctors agreed that all of the calculations and measurements were perfect, as were the purple marks and the fit of the mask. They studied their notes together and separately one additional time and did not leave the room until everything was checked and re-checked, measured and re-measured, and they were all in agreement that everything was perfect.

The overhead lights were turned on and off several more times, and each time the red laser beams were studied for the accuracy of their position as they reflected onto Ben's body. Chuck and I watched with fascination as the girls measured and re-measured with a variety of precise instruments. They worked together like the components of a finely crafted grandfather clock. Each person was like a perfectly calibrated moving part with her speed, actions, rhythms, and interactions with the others all being synchronous and flawless. It made me feel confident that all was progressing as smoothly as planned and that we would be ready to start the radiation as scheduled. This team knew what they were doing, and they did it well.

They finally finished their tedious work with a complete radiation rehearsal, and after they were fully satisfied, they let us go for the evening. While we were dressing Ben, one of the girls disappeared for a few minutes. We were just about through saying our good-byes and giving hugs and kisses when she came back into the room dragging a giant, black trash bag behind her. We were a bit perplexed wondering what she was doing but then realized that the bag was completely full of toys. Ben was given the opportunity to select a toy for himself and one for his little sister. They told us that they had not enjoyed their work so much in a long time, and they were very thankful to have met Ben and us. It made me feel so good because three hours ago, we were perfect strangers to them and just another job, yet now we were leaving as friends. No, we were now family. We had touched their lives, and they had certainly touched ours. It was a wonderful feeling leaving that department having made a difference in someone's day.

Ben held the two new toys, one under each arm, as we walked out to our car. I whispered to Chuck that I believed that God was using Ben for some great things. I believed that maybe we were going to be a witness of strength, faith, and the love of Jesus to a lot of people throughout this challenge of ours. What had just happened with the radiation technicians was supposed to be strictly medicine and business, but it had turned out to be so much more.

Chuck smiled, kissed me on the cheek, and put his arm over my shoulders. "I do too, honey," he said. "This is happening for a reason, and I feel we're going to be just fine."

●●●

A Test of Faith

The nurse had given us an information packet that was designed to answer any questions we might have about the actual irradiation treatment that we were about to begin. As usual, the information dwelled on the negatives and possible side effects of the treatment, all of which concerned me. I did not feel I was mentally ready to embark on another treatment that could potentially make Ben feel awful. He was doing remarkably well, so the thought of disturbing that state was depressing.

The nurse highlighted verbally that we should try to increase Ben's water intake because the side effects might be slightly minimized if he was adequately hydrated. When I returned to the apartment, I read through the literature provided and learned that this treatment could cause dry mouth, mouth sores, thick saliva, throat sores, and some dental problems. As I read through this list, I felt confident. These effects sounded manageable and probably not too uncomfortable for Ben, but as the nurse had recommended, I started pushing the water on him. He drank so much water the night prior to commencing radiation treatment that I am surprised his belly did not stick out as if he were nine months pregnant. We could do this, I thought. Radiation will be uneventful. We can get through it unscathed.

I continued reading the list. I learned that radiation could also cause skin irritation with burning, weight loss, moderate-to-severe nausea and vomiting, fatigue, diarrhea, and pain. My concerns began to surface again, but I still had a sense of power and control over the treatments. This sense of well-being and control paled and withered as I finished reading the chapter on side effects. The treatment could also cause a severe and life-threatening liver condition called "veno-occlusive disease," and it could also increase the risk of infection, which could be life threatening in the immune-suppressed patient. The last two potential side effects on the list were cataracts and infertility. I hardly noticed these last two possibilities because I was still so focused on the potentially deadly ones. Once again, I felt completely vanquished. I was defeated in the battle.

It took me all night to repair my spirits for Ben's benefit and to prepare myself for the next day. By morning, I was refreshed and energized and again felt deeply in my heart that God would watch over us and keep Ben safe. I had trusted His will thus far, and through the intensity of my prayers all night, I felt that I was not going to be let down at this point. I was convinced that He still had a great plan for this little boy, and I just had to get that idea through my thick head. It was virtually impossible to do, but I had to somehow not worry.

That didn't happen. I worried.

Radiation took a total of seven days, and it went perfectly. I should have listened to the scriptures, which read: ***"Do not be anxious about anything, but in everything, by prayer and petition, with thanksgiving, present your requests to God. And the peace of God, which transcends all understanding, will guard your hearts and your minds in Christ Jesus."*** (Philippians 4:6,7). I should not have been worried.

At first, Ben had huge, petrified eyes, but soon he was comfortable and at complete ease with the situation. The technicians, Chuck, Ben, and I all entered a large room where the treatments were to take place. I lifted Ben up onto the cold metal table and then stepped back while a young woman strapped Ben's body down with large, black Velcro straps. He did not flinch. The technicians, three of them, were all great with Ben. They asked him questions, and he answered and then proceeded to enlighten them with all of his detailed stories. Most of the stories were the same ones that he had shared with the simulation crew. These girls, like the others, were instantly captivated by Ben's personality and angelic disposition. I wished all of these girls could see him at home sometime when he was acting like a normal, untamed three-year-old. Nonetheless, that day he had them charmed, and me, too.

After he was positioned with the Velcro straps and had his head secured to the table via his new "hockey mask," we were all required to leave the room. The tech flipped off the overhead lights as we left, and the room changed from an intensively bright examination area to a dimly lit, comfortable environment. I was certain that Ben would panic and cry out for Chuck, but he didn't. He stayed perfectly still throughout the treatment course, which amazed me. We explained to him that we would be right outside the door and that we would be watching him on a small television set. A microphone was positioned near him so that we would be able to hear him speak to us, and so that he could respond to any questions or directions the staff might have during the treatment.

A Test of Faith

The door that separated us from Ben was massive and imposing. It stood eight feet tall, floor to ceiling, and was just over four inches thick. There was a solid, heavy handle that resembled the handle on the door of the safe at our local bank. Nothing could pass through that door. I was certain that it was even bullet proof.

We waited at the dose administration station with the technicians. We watched Ben on the TV screen and noticed that his eyes were looking straight up to the ceiling. His gaze seemed fixed. I would have given almost anything to know what he was thinking at that time. I'm not sure what I would have been thinking, but it probably would have been something about being scared.

The girl in charge of the treatment asked Ben if he was ready. "Hi, Ben. Can you hear us?" she said over the intercom.

I could hear his little voice reply, "Yes."

The technician told him that he would hear a soft engine running and that he would see the red laser beam that he had seen during the simulation service the day before. Ben seemed fine with this news.

"Hi, Ben, it's me, Mom. You're doing so well. Hold still, son," I said confidently. "In just a few seconds, you are going to hear the engine start, so hold perfectly still."

I could see his acknowledgment of my words in the very slight nod that the secured hockey mask would allow. We continued to talk over the intercom about how great he was doing, and we encouraged him, over and over again, to hold perfectly still. We counted down the seconds until the engine hum would cease and the beam of rays finished their lethal program. When the buzzer sounded, we announced that Ben could scratch his nose or "get the wiggles out." He was incredible.

The radiation treatment was explained to me this way: a normal x-ray for a person involves about 1000 rays of electromagnetic radiation of extremely short wave length and high penetrating power shined on the body for a fraction of a second. Radiation treatment to kill cancer cells is six million rays of moderate length and high penetrating power held on one spot for a full minute or more. Because this intensive dose of cell-killing light is so inconceivably destructive to human tissue, it is absolutely imperative that the beams touch only the spots intended; otherwise, healthy tissue will be instantly destroyed. For this reason, protective lead shields were everywhere, including inside the core of the door and all of the walls. Lead blocks were also positioned around Ben's body to further ensure the correct direction of these beams during treatment and to protect his healthy tissue. Only the two spots on his skull and his lower left abdomen where the tumor had grown were to be touched by the intense beams.

Each treatment took approximately forty-five minutes. We received the radiation doses at 9:15 a.m. and then again at 3:15 p.m. for seven consecutive days. In between sessions, blood work was drawn to ensure safe red and white blood cell counts, and we were encouraged to let Ben rest. He had no interest in the latter. He continued to laugh, run around, and play hockey. He didn't appear to be injured or affected in any way by the radiation. He did not experience even one side effect.

It was miraculous.

19

The Green Mask

Two weeks before admission to the hospital for the bone marrow transplant, Ben had to begin wearing a green surgical mask whenever he left the apartment. It was unusual to not be able to see his smile. We could only see his eyes as they peeked out from above the mask. It was obvious when he was smiling, though, for his eyes were bright and the part of his face that you could see lit up like sunshine. You could tell without a doubt when Ben was smiling, and he smiled a lot. Thank God that he was getting through this traumatic experience and was able to keep his beautiful disposition! He had peace in his heart, and he had security in us. I was thankful and proud to be his mom.

The idea of the mask was for Ben to be exposed to as few germs as possible. The risk of a cold, flu, or other bug from another person was too great; therefore, no more public exposure. We were banned from going to restaurants, malls, and even church. We could not go anywhere near a crowd. The restrictions gave us a glimpse of the many months to come and prepared us for a long battle with germs. We suddenly felt isolated, alone, and empty even though we were all together. It was as if the doctors had ordered our social life to be turned off from this moment on, and we felt a sense of abandonment. Although it was a difficult prescription to follow, we truly understood the importance and significance of keeping Ben as healthy as possible before he went into the hospital for the big punch.

We had come so far along. We were technically ready for the transplant but had to wait two weeks to give Ben's body a chance to rest, recover, and grow strong again after enduring the effects of the radiation. The kidneys had to have a chance to function normally without toxins or x-ray blasts so that Ben's body would be ready for the chemotherapy portion of the transplant. His body had to have the ability to flush out the massive doses of chemotherapy to come, and his kidneys were key in this process.

We were two weeks away from our biggest hurdle. Actually, it was more than a hurdle: this was going to be a family pole vault! We were ready to get this transplant underway but had mixed emotions. On one hand, we were bubbling with anticipation, but on the other, we were scared to death.

Dr. Driscoll met with us and reviewed the next steps. He told us that these two weeks would go by quickly, so he advised us to enjoy our time together before we would be separated in the transplant unit. He was very serious when he said this, and it made Chuck and me both very uncomfortable. I began to squirm in my chair, roll my shoulders back and forth, and rub my hands together nervously.

He noticed our uneasiness. "Ok, now relax for a few minutes," he said. "I have some very good news for you."

He told us that every one of Ben's tests and studies from the previous weeks had come back indicating PERFECT ranges for every function. He was especially surprised and thrilled that all kidney function was normal. He said that he had never seen this type of full recovery in the kidneys after this rough neuroblastoma protocol and that his plan was to go full force on the dose of pre-transplant chemotherapy. He was convinced that Ben would be able to handle the full dose of chemotherapy that would obliterate his entire immune system. He felt that we were going into this most difficult step with both feet firmly planted. He was excited for the potential of success, and so were we.

After receiving this good news in the doctor's office that afternoon, we left the hospital and jumped up and down with joy. We took pictures, hugged, whooped, and hollered. We yelled "Hooray!" and, as always, gave each other the sporting high-five hand slap.

The hospital's employee assigned to valet duty was stationed outside the front door of the children's clinic and was patiently waiting for his next customer. When he noticed our dancing and cheering, he watched curiously and reacted with a subdued grin. He probably at first thought that we had gone a little mad, but then I think he realized that we must have just received some very good news because it wasn't long before he joined in our celebration. He howled like a wolf and clapped his hands with us.

"Hee-ha!" Ben yelled back.

We thanked God again for getting us to this point, and we praised Him as we spun in circles and skipped a few steps. Yet, all the while

A Test of Faith

we were celebrating Dr. Driscoll's good news, Chuck and I were still deep down scared to death. Transplant was coming soon.

For two weeks we waited. We sat around the apartment and read books, played games, baked cookies, played volleyball with balloons, colored, had pillow fights, and grew very stir crazy. We became so edgy and impatient with each other in the tiny apartment that we had to get out. We needed fresh air and civilization. We were going bonkers, so we decided that our big outing would be to go for a walk in Duke's forest. Miss Patty, Lisa, Chuck, Dana, Ben, and I went for long walks in the morning and in the evening. Ben wore his mask, and we also had him wear rubber gloves. We could not take the chance that he would touch a rock or a tree that had a mold or fungus on it that could possibly become embedded under a fingernail or into a break in his skin. We took every precaution to protect Ben from the normal world around us, and we used every safeguard to keep him impeccably healthy during those two weeks.

Dr. Driscoll was right: the time went by very quickly. We were glad that we had carefully followed his prescription and had enjoyed every second of every day together.

20

Packing

At Duke University, the days of a bone marrow transplant were numbered. This way, everyone could keep track of what was happening along the timeline of recovery. The actual day of the infusion of the new cells, or transplant day, was called Day 0 (zero), so the days before 0 were –1, -2, -3, etc. We were officially at Day –8 when we were admitted onto the transplant unit. That meant that we had eight days to go before the actual infusion of the stem cells that had been harvested many weeks before. These were the same cells that were being stored somewhere at Duke, just waiting for the order to go back into Ben.

> June 27, 2001 Day -8

We were assigned to room 4 on the unit, which was located on the fifth floor of the main hospital building. When Miss Patty and Dana dropped us off at the front entrance of the hospital, I felt as though I were being sent away on a journey that would not allow me to ever talk to or see loved ones again. I felt incredibly alone, lost, and brokenhearted. In a matter of a few seconds, as I stood there on the curb, I felt every emotion of sadness and fear travel through me. When I hugged Miss Patty, I did not want to let go. I wanted to stay on that curb forever and not let her drive away, but we had to separate. I stood there, holding Ben's hand, while Chuck went to borrow the wagon from the reception desk, and I watched Miss Patty pull away with what seemed to be all of my security and strength.

We made our way through the hospital lobby to the main set of elevators located just past the small gift shop. Ben did not say anything as he watched all the activity of the busy lobby. We took the center elevator car to the fifth floor as we had been directed, and when the doors opened at our designated floor, we exited. We had to

A Test of Faith

make a left turn, then a quick right, and continue until we faced a brightly painted, purple hallway. At the end of this hallway was the bone marrow transplant unit.

The hallway was fifty yards long, and, all things considered, it was a relatively pleasant walk. A variety of framed artwork decorated both sides of the hallway, and each art project was unique, creative, and very colorful. These masterpieces of design and imagination were from the hearts of young children from elementary schools in the Durham area. I was surprised to find myself looking at every picture as we made our way down the hall. I suppose I was trying to relish our last few moments of precious freedom, for the walk we were taking was leading us to the place where we would remain isolated for at least the next five weeks. I guess I was trying to stall the inevitable as long as I could. I knew that after we passed through the doors ahead of us, we were in store for a very long and grueling medical procedure. It was what the doctors had forewarned us would be the most difficult and risky part of Ben's treatment.

As we made our way down the narrow pass, Ben sat comfortably in the borrowed wagon. The high-sided, green, durable wagon was similar to other products produced by a recognizable company to us. In the past, we had used the company's children's jungle gyms, climbing stations, and even portable high chairs. Ben was very content to go for a ride in this useful and familiar toy. He sat comfortably in the wagon, although he was mostly hidden by all of the stuff that we were allowed to bring with us into our transplant room.

We had received a welcome packet from Duke about two months prior to our arrival. In the packet were all of the rules that had to be obeyed while on the unit. One section went into great detail about what was recommended to bring along and what was not. We were advised to buy an under-the-bed plastic storage bin, which I easily found at a Target store. In this flat plastic box, we were to pack everything needed for the next month or so.

There were specific directions given on how to pack the things we were bringing, and it took me two full weeks to pack just as they had recommended. I had to wash Ben's clothes twice in the hottest water available using a detergent with bleach. Each doubly washed article of clothing then had to be placed into a Ziploc bag. For convenience, I decided to pack a full outfit into each particular Ziploc: shorts, T-shirt, socks, and underwear. I did this over and over again for the clothes we were to have with us. I packed several pairs of pajamas, and then, per their recommendation, I bought six really fun and bright pillowcases. They included Scooby-Doo, Blue's Clues, trains, cars, and sports, of course. Just like everything else, these had to be washed twice and packed individually into Ziploc bags.

I wanted to pack a few toys and some snacks, too, because nothing was provided on the floor. The rules for these items were also very strict. Each toy had to be relatively new and thoroughly wiped down with a bleach and water solution. After it had completely dried, the toy had to go into the famous Ziploc. It was a good thing that I had gone to the local Sam's Club and purchased a load of gallon-sized plastic bags.

Organizing the snack situation was another part of my packing project. No snack was allowed to be perishable, and no fresh fruit was allowed. We were under specific orders to feed Ben processed food only. At first, I was uncomfortable with this idea as I was always one to feed the children healthy, fresh, unprocessed food. It made sense that the least amount of preservatives in the diet would promote the best health. The orders for the transplant unit, however, were completely the opposite. Only processed foods were allowed because we could know for certain that no live bacteria, fungus, or other harmful organisms were being brought onto the unit.

Every snack also had to be packaged in individual servings. We were not allowed to open anything and have it exposed in the room for longer than thirty minutes. If Ben did not finish eating or drinking in that time frame, the food or drink had to be thrown away. It took me a long time in the grocery store, but I finally found everything I needed: tiny bags of Goldfish, individual boxes of Cheerios, juice bags with wrapped straws, mini bags, lunch size, of a variety of chips, individual packets of Gummy Bears, and others. By the time I finished shopping, there really was a good choice and variety of foods for a little boy.

I followed further instructions about the packing of snack food. I was surprised at the orders, but I took the advice very seriously and did what I was told to do. I wiped down the outside of each package with the bleach and water mix, waited for the package to dry, and then, again, put the box, bag or packet into a Ziploc bag.

A Test of Faith

Everything I packed was as sterile and free of germs as it could possibly be. I felt really good about how I had packed. I was sure of myself and convinced that every item I planned to take into Ben's sterile room was germ free. These packages, clothes, toys, and snacks were cleaner than they had ever been before, and I felt confident in allowing them near my son.

Germs. We live with them all the time, so who would ever think that such a big deal had to be made of them? I was trying to figure it out while I was doing all of this preparatory work for our admission. It did not take long at all to realize how important cleanliness was now and what it meant to be really clean. Normally, we can fight off just about anything that comes in contact with our bodies. If, however, a germ or microorganism that has the possibility to become a pathogen comes into contact with the right body part at the right time, an illness will develop. For example, if people sneeze into their hands and then shake the hands of others, their cold germs will spread from hand to hand. If those people, in turn, touch their mouths or noses, the germs will enter their respiratory systems and have a heyday. Each recipient of a handshake then has the workings of a full-blown cold. The germ (and the illness) will continue to grow and fester because it will be quite active in the host body. If a person who gets the new germ does not have the ability to fend off or fight that newly forming illness, he or she could die. During the bone marrow transplant, the body is depleted of its entire immune system. Therefore, any germ on that transplant unit could potentially be fatal to any one of the kids, not just ours.

To further protect the unit from any germs, before we could enter, we first had to pass through the "anteroom." The thirty-foot long room had two thick doors, one at each end. The first door connected us to the main, purple hall with all of the kids' artwork, and the other door permitted us to pass into the unit. The doors could not be opened at the same time because of a positive pressure system built in to prevent any germs from the outside hallway getting into the unit. There was a square metal button on the wall to the right just outside that hallway door. We first had to peek into the window to be sure that the inside door was closed before we could get this outside door to open.

Inside the anteroom, we were required to scrub our hands and forearms with a special soap for a full thirty seconds. Thirty seconds didn't seem very long at first, but as the weeks passed, those thirty seconds seemed to be forever. A clock with a bold second hand was mounted above the sink so that nobody could make the mistake of misjudging the time. The soap dispenser and the water faucet were both controlled by foot pedals located on the floor at the base of the sink cabinet.

On our first day, we were nervous about passing through that second door, so we scrubbed and scrubbed, rubbing between each finger and soaping up to our elbows. We scrubbed even though a line started to form behind us. Parents who looked like zombies were waiting outside to scrub before they could re-enter the unit to return to the child they most certainly loved as dearly as we loved Ben. So, we scrubbed for the required time and then added a few extra seconds just to be sure that every germ and any germ was completely gone from our hands before we dried them. The paper towel system was set up to have the towel ready for use, so there was no need to turn a crank or push a lever. It was designed to prevent clean hands from being contaminated.

The hand washing procedure was strictly enforced, and every single person who was to pass through the second door was required to wash as thoroughly as possible. Even if the person just had a simple delivery to make on the unit, he or she had to stop and scrub. I was impressed with the setup and obeyed the orders posted on every wall, inside and outside of that anteroom. The orders were so tremendously important to the well-being of the fragile bodies on the other side that I couldn't possibly imagine disobeying them.

When we were ready to actually go inside onto the unit, we first had to get the inside door to open. Again, on the wall to the right, we found a blue, square entry button similar to the one used to get into this anteroom in the first place. I always pushed this inside button with my elbow. I wanted my hands to be perfectly sterile before I went anywhere on that unit. This was my responsibility. It was a big one that was going to protect my son's life.

Inside the unit, the atmosphere was intense. Anyone who entered instantly realized the seriousness of the situation at hand. Saving lives was an extremely delicate process, and saving lives was what these people were all about. When the inside door closed firmly behind us, everything seemed suddenly quiet. It was as if we had walked in on a funeral service where people were reflecting deeply on the subject of

A Test of Faith

death. I hated it that first day. My heart pounded in my chest, and my palms started sweating. I didn't know what else my body could do to prepare me for the "fight or flight" response. I wanted someone to laugh or talk or do something to break the tension; I wanted to turn around with Ben in my arms and run. Instead, I drew in a deep breath and then slowly exhaled through pursed lips.

Before I was able to exhale all of the air in my lungs, a young, smiling nurse greeted Chuck, Ben, and me. She was dressed in a colorful set of scrubs decorated with Looney Tune characters holding stethoscopes and clipboards. I was relieved to see her smile and hear her warm welcome, but I was still very uncomfortable. I was also more scared than I had never been before.

21

The Unit

A bone marrow transplant unit is an intensive care unit, plain and simple. Our room was one of sixteen available along the left side of an "L"-shaped, 8-foot-wide hallway that was about 300 feet long. There was a main nurse's station at the bend of the "L," and there were mini nurse's stations outside of each and every room. Each room had a closed door with a window and another small window to the side of the door. A computer was set up outside of each patient's door, and it was equipped with a monitor to display all of the vital statistics that were being closely measured inside the room. A small workstation was mounted on the wall outside the room's entry. A bottle of alcohol-based, foam soap mounted on the outside doorframe hung upside down and ready for use. Before people entered any room, they had to foam up their hands with the germ-killing soap. It was another precaution taken to be certain that no germ would come near the patient.

Our room was number 4. Usually I'm not one for favorite numbers, flowers, or even colors because I like everything, but for some unknown reason, the number 4 felt good. I was glad to be assigned to that room number, however crazy it sounded.

On the outside of the door was a small, dry erase board that had written on it, "Welcome Benjamin." I smiled when I saw the welcome and sighed with relief when we met our coordinator, Carmen, who had written it. She was bright eyed and smiled as she greeted us and introduced us to our room. She wore white pants and a collared, pink, button-down shirt. On top of her outfit was an extremely clean, pressed, long white lab coat. She wore her Duke nametag hanging from the left collar, and on the nametag were many pins. I liked the little angel and the "thumbs up" pin. Chuck and I both wondered if she was brand new to the unit because her lab coat was in such perfect shape. Chuck decided that either she was, in fact, on her very first day

A Test of Faith

of work, or she really did not do any work. He teased her about this from the start, and it became a running joke with the two of them. We said hello and good-bye to Carmen, after which she went on her way to the next new family. A nurse showed us how to use the foam hand wash, and we all foamed up our hands and rubbed the soap in. Then we entered our room.

There was a large piece of plastic, very similar to a thick Saran Wrap, lying on the bed and covering the pillow. When the room was cleaned for Ben, this was part of the protocol that gave a bit of insurance that the blanket and pillow would not collect any dust particles while waiting for us to arrive. When the nurse opened the door of the room for us and we all went in, she immediately removed the plastic so that Ben could sit down on his bed. Above him was the typically bright fluorescent light bulb seen in hospital rooms, and when it was turned on, the entire bed was so well lit that you could see the smallest speck of even a loose white thread anywhere on the white linens. It was overpowering but served a great purpose during an exam of Ben's skin, eyes, or any other part of his body.

Mounted on the wall beside the bed were a number of pieces of equipment. There was a monitor to keep track of Ben's heart and lung function, a blood pressure cuff, his own ear thermometer, a pulse oxymeter to measure oxygen levels in his blood, several oxygen outlets, special plugs, and bags of equipment, plastic tubing, emergency apparatus, and more. Beside the bed was a tall IV pole with an attached electronic medication pump for administering drugs.

We looked around the room and out the window as we settled the box of clothes, toys, and snacks under the bed. I was glad to have followed the advice of the manual with the under-the-bed box because the room was too small for anything else. It measured about eleven feet by eleven feet overall, but it was not completely square. There was a tiny bathroom off to the side and a Murphy bed that dropped down from the wall next to the bathroom. This was where Chuck or I would sleep.

The pull-down bed was about half the size of a regular twin bed, so it was pretty small and about impossible (we found out later) to roll over in. You had to actually do a three-step, roll-over-in-place type of motion: lying on your right side, lift but don't dare roll, flip to the back, lift again but don't roll, and flip to the left side. If a change of position had been attempted any other way, we would certainly have rolled off the bed onto the floor. There was not much room on the floor, however, so we would have almost landed directly on top of Ben. Chuck had a really rough time with this narrow bed because he is bigger than I am. I was also able to stretch out on the bed, but Chuck, being 5'11" tall, had to stay in the fetal position all night. There was no room for him to straighten out his body on the short mattress, and the mattress was the exact length to fit between two walls.

Above the miniature bed was a nice-sized window that overlooked a pretty courtyard and garden five stories below. The flowers were in beautiful bloom as they surrounded a small sitting area of benches. The roses, chrysanthemums, sunflowers, daisies, petunias, and crocuses were fabulous. The few benches were occupied by a small number of people, and others walked slowly along the flower-lined sidewalk. Most of the people were dressed in white coats or surgical scrubs, but some just wore plain street clothes. They seemed to be enjoying their lunches and had no awareness of what our family was about to embark upon right above them.

It took me about twenty minutes to decorate the room with some memorable pictures and a lot of color. My goal was to soften the intense institutional atmosphere by adding a personal touch and providing a comfortable feeling of home. I put up a big picture of Mickey Mouse and a smaller picture of Dana and Ben hugging.

I also set an eight-by-ten-inch framed picture of Jesus on the wheeled bed table, and as I did so, I asked Him to be very close to us. I invited Him to sit at Ben's bed and to have angels stand guard at the door. I prayed that He would refuse any germ admittance into this room. I pleaded for His mercy on what was to come for little Ben's body, and finally, I reminded God that He had promised me many weeks ago that He would restore health unto Ben, that He would heal him. I told Jesus that if anyone could do this, it would be He, and I prayed for His will.

"Please, Dear God, with all of my heart and soul, I ask and trust that you will heal my son," I prayed softly. I kissed Jesus' picture as I set it down. As I did this, I heard Ben saying a prayer, too.

"Yeah, Jesus, please get rid of all the bad guy cells so that we can go back home."

I decorated the outside of Ben's door, too. I put his name up in big, bold letters and surrounded it with several family pictures of better times, happier times, and healthier times. I wanted everyone who walked by to see what our family looked like. I wanted them to know us and to know Ben as a healthy, playful, and energetic big brother to Dana. I wanted them to meet the family that soon would be cured of this cancer and would be doing normal things together, especially the simple things in life that I missed so much.

Because the bathroom, and the room in general, for that matter, were for Ben only, Chuck and I were given a locker down the hall and around the corner in the parent lounge. The rules stated that parents could not use the bathroom in the patient's room, nor could they eat or drink in the room, and these rules were strictly enforced for the patient's safety. I felt at times as if I should not even breathe in the room, but that was all in my head. As long as I was perfectly healthy, scrubbed properly, and used the foam soap, I was safe to enter. To provide extra security, I imposed on myself the rule of wiping down the bottom of my shoes with alcohol before entering because anything less than germ free was simply too dangerous of a risk to take for the patient, and the patient was my son.

Only one parent at a time was allowed to stay overnight with Ben, and this was another rule that was strictly enforced. There was not enough room in the small quarters for two adults and the medical staff who had to come in. They frowned on two parents in the room during the day, but we knew that we were probably going to have to break that rule. If we got in the way, we would leave; otherwise, we both had to be there. It was going to be one of those experiences that if you were not there to see with your own eyes, you would go crazy trying to imagine how things were going. It was just so much less stressful to be able to see Ben breathing firsthand, to see the monitor of his heartbeat firsthand, and to answer to his needs firsthand.

The locker assigned to us in the parent lounge was nothing like the last locker assignment I had, which was in high school. Then, I had a locker that was slightly taller than I was. I had to stretch onto my tiptoes to be able to reach the books that I put on the top shelf of that locker. The locker assigned to us at Duke was one-third the size of my high school issue. This worked fine, though, as all we had to put into this small space were a couple of toothbrushes, some toothpaste, a hairbrush, mouthwash, a change of clothes, and a couple of snacks. Chuck had Peanut M & M's in his little basket, and I had an Oats and Honey granola bar.

Sandie Klassen

    I felt sorry for the parents who did not have a spouse to switch off nights, or those who did not have an apartment to go to once in a while. Those moms and dads had to literally live out of that locker. They had to have everything they would need for a long time stuffed into that very small space. One guy had to contort his body to prevent things from falling out whenever he tried to close the locker door because it was so packed with clothes, toiletries, slippers, and socks.

    There was one toilet and one shower in the lounge for all of us parents to share. A washer and dryer, refrigerator, microwave, stove, sink, and some shelves were also provided. Each shelf was seven inches tall, one foot deep, and a-foot-and-a-half wide, and each was marked with our room number. Any food that the parent might need could be stored on this assigned shelf. I was grateful for the accommodations made for the parents, but my plan was to go there only to use the toilet; otherwise, my plan was to never leave Ben's side while on my shift. I would eat meals only when I was back at the apartment with Dana, Miss Patty, and Lisa on the days when it was Chuck's turn at the hospital. The rest of the time, I would live on occasional snacks of crunchy Cheetos or Goldfish eaten rapidly at the parent table while Ben was asleep. My job was going to be to stay at Ben's side every second to be sure that he was feeling safe, secure, and comfortable and to properly attend to his needs. Believe it or not, that is exactly what I did.

22

Pre-Transplant

After we settled into our room, Chuck and I finally sat down to relax. Ben was comfortable on his hospital bed and was playing with the bed's control panel.

"Look, you guys, this bed has the same buttons as my bed at Dr. Salman's hospital," he said joyfully.

I smiled at him as I stood to put some final touches on my decorating. The last steps needed to be fully suited to our new room were to put the Winnie the Pooh pillowcase onto Ben's hospital-issued pillow and to neatly fold his sterile fire truck blanket at the foot of the bed.

Ben was fine. He was so used to hospital rooms by this time that they all seemed the same to him. His only concern for the moment was if the VCR worked and if this hospital had "*Skip Dog*." He laughed and told stories to Chuck and me as we sat and tried our best to look as if we were listening intently. We nodded appropriately, giggled with him, and responded after a question was asked.

My mind wandered to thoughts of nurses and doctors and the "Consent for Treatment" papers I had signed just a few days earlier. These were the consent papers that reported the risks of the bone marrow transplant. The risks were embedded in my memory, and they haunted me. The papers noted that side effects could include but not be limited to nausea, vomiting, and hair loss; mucositis, an irritation of the lining of the mouth and digestive system, which can lead to mouth pain and ulcers, difficulty eating and swallowing, cramps, and diarrhea; low blood counts with risks of serious bleeding and infections and the need for transfusions and antibiotics; damage to the lungs, which could be fatal; and reactions that could result in low blood pressure or cardiac arrest. Side effects could also include severe itching and possibly swelling of the face, hands, and feet; severe allergic reaction with difficulty breathing caused by swelling of the trachea or windpipe; loss of essential elements in the body, which could lead to severe muscle weakness and nerve irritation; hearing loss, kidney failure, and liver damage. Additionally, I had to sign that I understood the risks of pneumonia, severe lung infection, and death.

"So, all in all, do you understand what you are approving for us to do to your son?" they had asked. "Will you sign here so that we can be released of any liability should he die while undergoing this procedure?" they continued. "Here…initial each page, and sign on the dotted line."

I whispered to Chuck, "Why are we doing this? He's so healthy and perfect right now. Are we sure this has to be done?"

"I know," Chuck answered. "All of a sudden it doesn't seem like the right thing to do."

Chuck and I already knew the answer to our question about the need to go through with the transplant because we had asked the doctors this question over and over again. Dr. Driscoll said that the chances for a recurrence of the cancer were extremely high if we did not go through with the transplant. He admitted that he had had other parents who decided to forego this last step because they felt just as we did: their child looked and acted so perfectly healthy that the risks of the transplant itself did not seem worth it. But Dr. Driscoll advised us from his heart. He looked us both in the eye and said, "Please go through with it. If this were my son, there would be no question in my mind. Transplant is that important to curing neuroblastoma."

I knew all along that we would go the distance, but when Ben was dancing in the living room, when we were all in our pajamas playing pile-up on the floor, when he was eating his entire bowl of Cheerios, and when he was jumping, running, hiking, hugging, kissing, and being a pure joy, it was hard to plan to go forward with the trauma of a bone marrow transplant.

The nurse came in shortly after Chuck and I finished our conversation. Ben still had his full attention on the dog movie, so it hardly fazed him when the nurse entered. Chuck and I stood immediately. She was our first official visitor from the medical staff. We stood at attention when she entered the room almost as if she was a general in the army, and we were young cadets. She had her hands full of large bags of saline and what looked like miles of plastic tubing. She also had a sweet smile on her face.

Ben finally turned his attention to her and let out a confident and bold, "Hi!"

Her business manner melted, and she stood for a long time talking to Ben before she began her nursing duties. She chatted with him about the pictures on the outside of his door and about his little sister. She asked him about his pillowcase and if Pooh Bear was his favorite of all the Disney characters. She asked what he liked best about the fire trucks and if he had ever seen one up close. She was so smooth. She was a total natural with this little three-year-old as she showed genuine interest in his side of the conversation.

Ben went on and on with his usual, "...and you know what?" before going into the details of his personal story. I couldn't help but smile and fill my lungs with the pure air. I was completely full of pride and love for this little boy. He was great. For a moment, I was lost in time.

The nurse then put on a mask and gloves and began her duties. She hung the water on the IV pole and secured two different caps to the ends of Ben's garden hoses. She ran the plastic tubing through a square pump that was mounted to the lower half of the pole. She took Ben's blood pressure, temperature, and pulse. She performed a full physical examination, which included a study of the inside of his mouth. She looked into his eyes and ears and then tickled his feet. He let out a huge laugh and pulled his feet up reflexively. They got along famously, which was a relief to us. She ended up being our primary nurse, and we were delighted to have the assignment.

The water bag had to drip into Ben for a full twenty-four hours. This step was called "hydration," and it was designed to increase the water content in Ben's body so that there would be adequate fluids to be able to flush out the chemotherapy that was to come. When this hydration period was completed, he would be ready to start the struggle of transplant. In addition to the water solution, or saline, several preparatory and prophylactic medications were also put through the pump and into the garden hoses. We came to know these drugs well and made ourselves a schedule so that we would know what to expect and when.

We had learned from the past eight months that it was imperative for us to be Ben's advocates. We were the ones to check and double-check that what he was receiving was truly intended for him. We were the ones to ensure that the medicines were given on time, and we were the ones to ensure that nothing was ever forgotten. The clock was again ticking, and we were on duty.

23

96 Hours of Destruction

June 28, 2001 Day -7

The infusion of the chemotherapy started at precisely 3:30 p.m. A team of nurses had to come in together to start this "conditioning regime." They were dressed in what resembled full chemical warfare gear, which shocked me. I thought that this must be terribly frightening to Ben, so we immediately began teasing the team.

"Look, Ben, three astronauts," we told him.

Ben liked space ships and astronauts, but astronomy and space were not his first love. He had a T-shirt that said, "When I grow up, I want to be an astronaut," and he had some pajamas with rocket ships all over them, but, in reality, he really did not want much to do with rocket ships or the planets. I had bought the pajamas on sale, and my Aunt Pat, who works for NASA, had given him the shirt. I think it is her secret dream for Ben to become a cosmonaut. She may be disappointed unless his interests change.

Each nurse wore a full white jumpsuit, shoe covers, masks with eye shields, and special hats that covered their foreheads and ears. They did not wear the normal latex gloves, but rather had on heavy-duty rubber gloves similar to the kind that I had worn in the past to clean my oven.

It was against the rules for just one nurse to do the job of hanging the chemotherapy drugs. It was a safety issue, and this precaution was one that I was especially happy that Duke had adopted. We were told that Ben would receive chemotherapy for ninety-six consecutive hours. This chemotherapy would be given in extremely high doses and would therefore kill as many malignant cells as possible. It would completely destroy all of Ben's bone marrow and, hence, was called "high dose marrow ablative therapy."

Because these drugs were so powerful, they would, of course, also destroy normal cells in Ben's body. The doctor promised that the chemotherapy was going to make Ben very, very sick. In fact, after the ninety-six hours of chemotherapy, Ben would not be able to recover on his own. The doses they were going to give him were lethal. If the stem cells that we harvested in April were not ready for re-infusion, Ben would die. There was no way that his bone marrow could begin to form blood again on its own. He would need clean bone marrow cells put back into him, and we would hope, pray, and wait until they engrafted and grew. "Engraftment" meant that the cells basically built themselves a home and would continue to live, multiply, and function.

Therefore, I was more than pleased to see the nurses come into the room as a group. I was glad for the system of safety checks in preparation for this brew of chemicals to begin dripping into my son.

Chuck and I sat and watched closely as the very reluctant drip began to appear in the plastic tube and make its way toward Ben's heart. It literally happened in slow motion. I studied the hose. I watched and waited. My heart was racing. My eyes filled with tears, but I was able to catch them at the corner of my eye before they could fall onto my cheek. I wiped quickly and repeated this motion over and over again.

Ben noticed and asked, "What's wrong, Mommy? Why are you crying?"

I could not bear to tell the truth that I was scared to death for him. Instead, I did what I always said I would never do—I lied to him.

"I'm so happy," I said. "This is the magic medicine that is going to get rid of that bad guy cell forever."

Ben sat up tall, looked up at the medicine, and then looked back at Chuck and at me. He smiled and said, "Yeah, Mom, this medicine is going to punch that bad guy cell out forever!"

24

A Very Sick Boy

> June 29, 2001 Day -6

We had been in the hospital at Duke for two full days, but I wasn't quite sure if it felt like two or more like twenty. The medical equipment necessary for Ben's care was trickling in, and as the nursing staff brought each new piece into the small room, our precious space dwindled even further. We began to feel as if we were a family of seven living in a ten-by-ten-foot motor home. It was much too early in our journey to start feeling cramped, but I couldn't help it.

Nothing about the room was capacious. Every time I turned around, I was either bumping my head on the low shelf that held the oxymeter and blood pressure cuff, or I was banging my hip on Ben's bedside table while trying to pass to the opposite side of the room to tend to Ben's needs. The door to the bathroom could not be left open because there was not enough room; when open, the door hit the corner of the bed and left no passable path from one side of the bed to the other.

As the chemotherapy slowly dripped into Ben's body, he began to feel its effects with a great deal of nausea. The doctors added more drugs to his order sheet with hopes of combating the miserable feeling of which Ben was constantly complaining. He could not overcome the relentless sensation of needing to vomit, but remarkably, his spirits remained positive and inspiring to us all.

I hoped that a change of scenery would distract Ben from his unsettled stomach, so I suggested a trip to visit his nurses at the nurse's station. He responded with great affirmation and enthusiasm, so we masked up and went into the hallway. We played a mini game of hockey at the end of the corridor. He also rode a little tricycle for an amazing total of seven laps. Every time we passed by the nurse's station, Ben waved and the staff cheered. We had a good time and were out of the room for over an hour without once needing the bucket. I was relieved that when we were in the hallway, nothing seemed as depressing as it had on that very first day. The funeral had ended as far as I was concerned, and we were going to bring joy and laughter to the halls.

When we returned to our room, we scrubbed our hands, forearms, and elbows with the foam wash and wrote a message on our dry erase board. We wrote, "Jesus loves me," and signed it, "Ben."

Three more days of the constant chemotherapy drip, and Ben's immune system would be completely obliterated. Just the thought of the impending effects hovered over me like a dark rain cloud. I was literally watching as the drugs slowly killed my son. They were working to debilitate Ben's body. Now, as much as always, we needed to continue to pray, "Please be with us, Lord. Don't dare leave us now."

June 30, 2001 Day -5

Ben was violently sick from the moment the day theoretically started, which was midnight. The vomiting was fiercer than we had ever before experienced, and we had to get a third bucket to help with our cleaning routine. Chuck and I were bumping into each other as one of us tried to go into the bathroom to clean out the messy, vomit-filled bucket while the other was trying to get out of the bathroom and back to Ben's side to hold the next pail. Ben's eyes were heavy and bloodshot from the force of his efforts, and he was crying.

"I hate this!" he screamed. "I can't do this," he added through clenched teeth. He did not understand why he needed to suffer the way he was, and neither did we. At one point, he yelled to Chuck, "Please make this stop, Daddy! It hurts too much." And then he continued, "Please, Mommy, I hate this. Help me!"

We tried. We buzzed the nurse, and then we waited briefly for her response. When she was not at our room within seconds, one of us was out in the hallway tracking her down. Chuck and I even yelled at each other several times because we were feeling so helpless. It didn't take long before I lost control and yelled out loud, "Jesus, God, HELP us already!"

July 1, 2001 Day -4

Summer was supposed to be filled with fun times: picnics, pool parties, cookouts, and campouts were normal for most families this time of year. The celebration of our country's birth was rapidly approaching, but unfortunately, unlike most families, we were not planning on attending any fireworks display. Instead, we were counting down the minutes until this chemotherapy blast would end. We had completed seventy-two hours of the continuous drip of the baneful and inimical fluid. We were now beginning the last twenty-four hours, or 1440 minutes—the homestretch of this most frightening part of the bone marrow transplant.

While watching the minutes tick away and Benjamin grow more ill, we began to wonder how in the world we were ever going to make it through this process. The doctor, sounding too pessimistic for my taste, reported, "This is the easy part." I felt sick just hearing his words. I was in total disbelief, and I felt that there must be something more we could do to help Ben. He had been sick around the clock now, and Chuck and I were as exhausted as our baby was. We began to argue and share our less-than-likable sides with each other. Because of the rules, one of us had to leave, which we realized was best for our marriage at that moment anyway, so we decided together that Chuck would go home that night. I would stay at Ben's side.

I felt depleted of energy and emotion and had to fight feeling sorry for myself as I was not the one throwing up every ten minutes or less and being poisoned to death. This disease did not seem to care whom it hurt, and it was now more than ever hurting Ben and also Chuck, Dana, and me. I felt I was beginning to get trapped into a self-pitying, "why me" and "why us" attitude. I suddenly wanted to blame someone or somebody for this cancer. I was mad at God for not working His miracle faster and for allowing this to happen at all.

My attitude was no longer healthy, and I soon realized that having such a negative state of mind was going to do nothing but destroy all of us. I knew that I had to take the bull by the horns and face these trials bravely and with a positive outlook. I had to grab hold of this lousy bull with all of my might and throw it to the ground. I had to put my foot on its stunned body, raise my arms into the air, and yell out a grizzly roar. I had to find strength to be able to make it through my shift; I needed desperately to be focused and positive, for Ben's sake.

We had a break from 1:30 a.m. until almost 3:00 a.m. while my son slept. His body could take no more for the moment. Although his forehead was beaded with sweat, his body was otherwise spent. He had no choice but to sleep, but there was no way that I could. I did not sleep, but rather picked up the blue, child's-size stool that we had bought and pulled it up to his bedside. I sat down on it, rested my head in my hands on Ben's bed, and waited for the next go-round. I can't remember what I was thinking or if I even felt like praying. I just felt numb.

July 2, 2001 Day -3

The nurse pulled off the empty bag of Carboplatin chemotherapy at precisely 3:30 p.m. We had survived the four full days, exactly ninety-six hours, since the chemotherapy began dripping, and we were happy to see the last of the cancer-fighting drug disappear. I was relieved to see the nurse come into Ben's room, dressed again in her astronaut attire, and throw the empty bag and jumbled tubing into the large, yellow, hazardous materials bag. Chuck was at Ben's side, too, so with weak voices but powerful thoughts, we celebrated this milestone in our treatment.

I spoke softly and mostly to myself: "Good-bye, chemotherapy. Never again."

By early evening, Ben was feeling somewhat better and was sitting up in his bed. I am quite certain that he had absolutely no idea of the magnitude of what he had just experienced. He will not realize this until he is a grown man looking back on this time of his life, but I am confident that this crisis is something that I will never forget. The intensity of emotion that I experienced and the significance of every detail of this awful time will be forever embedded in my mind.

Great comfort came to me when I noticed Ben's nonchalance as he went back to his project at his bedside table. I realized that quite possibly these memories would soon escape his young mind. I had set up crayons and paper on his hospital tray and had it pulled up close to him. He was busy coloring and tracing the fingers of his left hand, and he seemed content with the evening. I felt weak in body, mind, and spirit, but relieved to see that Ben appeared unscathed by the past four days of torture.

A Test of Faith

The atmosphere in Ben's room was finally tranquil and at ease, and it made me feel safe and secure. It had been a long time since I had relaxed comfortably. This feeling of security lasted for nearly five hours, all of which I felt was earned and well deserved, and I was thankful for it.

By 11:00 p.m. I was ready for some good sleep. I needed to rest my mind and body. Ben was satisfied, and the lights were off. His fire truck blanket was tucked under his chin, and he slept so beautifully. I kissed his forehead and then climbed into my little bed. The room was never dark because the hallway illumination peeked through our blinds, and the room was never quiet because of the beeping pumps and monitors. We rested, though, very soundly for nearly an hour.

By midnight, the mucositis started to develop. The medical staff told us that the first sign that the chemotherapy was killing off bad cells, and a good sign, was that Ben would begin to develop mouth sores called "mucositis." At first they would be similar to little canker sores on the inside of his cheeks and under his tongue. Unfortunately, the entire digestive track would eventually develop these sores, so from mouth to anus, all internally, his body would be full of the most painful and vicious blisters that one could ever experience. Consequently, Ben would stop eating. This was normal, they said, and when it began to affect Ben's eating or drinking ability, the doctor would order an intravenous feeding program called "TPN" (total parenteral nutrition). This artificial feeding system was essential to keeping Ben alive and nourished while we waited until he could once again, independently, take in food and water.

We saw our first two mouth sores late into the night after the chemotherapy drip had come to an end. There was a small open pocket on the inside of his bottom lip on the right side. I figured it out when he woke up thirsty and asked for something to drink.

In a very sleepy voice, I asked, "What would you like to drink?"

"Orange juice, please."

I smiled at his manners so late in the night and under all of these unusual circumstances. We had some orange juice in the small refrigerator, so I peeled back the foil cover and placed a straw in the cup. He took a sip of the juice and immediately winced and cried out in pain. His outburst shook me, and within a second, I was fully awake. I turned on the soft overhead light and looked at him. He was wiggling in his bed as if his bottom was sitting on pins.

"What is it? What's wrong, Ben?"

"My mouth," he yelled. "It hurts."

I buzzed for the nurse, who arrived within seconds. She studied the inside of Ben's mouth with a flashlight until she was finally able to locate the first of the painful culprits. As soon as we knew what was wrong, we tried to persuade Ben to rinse the citrus juice out of his mouth with fresh water. He was hesitant but obeyed. Finally, he grew somewhat comfortable. Before long, he was once again asleep.

July 3, 2001 Day -2

Even though the mucositis caused some additional suffering, Ben continued to be stronger than the pain and to show interest in food. He had one-half of a peanut butter sandwich and some Pez candy. He ate an orange Popsicle and drank a small cup of ice water. He ate a few potato chips and then went back for more Pez. He concentrated as he tilted back the Mickey Mouse head to dispense the cherry-flavored candy.

Except for the usual antibiotic, antifungal, steroid, and fluid administration, and the constant attention of the medical staff, Ben was left alone for three days to give his body a chance to rest before they were to put in the good guy cells. This was Day one of the three. We had to hope that by Day three his white blood cell count would drop from its normal 10.0 down to a level of zero.

"Zero" meant that his body had no ability to fight infection. The doctors wanted the white count to be zero because that would be an indication that all of the bone marrow had been destroyed. It meant that the drugs had attacked every cell in Ben's marrow; the cancer would be gone, and the body would be ready for new life. To test the white blood cell count, each morning around 4:00 a.m., a nurse came in to take vital signs and draw two tubes of blood from Ben's central line. By 8:00 a.m., when the doctor began rounds, the blood work had returned from the lab and could be interpreted by the medical staff. This morning's report showed Ben's white count at .6, so it was, in fact, dropping as we expected and hoped. All was good. Great, actually.

Ben was slowing down quite a bit but still had some of his usual spunk and joyful spirit. He was eating and drinking less, but he still wanted to sit up in his bed. He laughed as we told "knock-knock" jokes, and he even let us give him a bath. At Duke, we always gave the bath standing so that his garden hoses with all of the lines attached would not get into the water.

In addition to keeping his body clean from all germs, we also had the responsibility of keeping his mouth clean. The nurse explained to him that the mouth has lots of "yucky" germs and that it was extremely important that Ben rinse his mouth and swab it out at least three times per day and always after he threw up. Each morning, a sterile cup of white solution and another of a pink solution was left on the fold-down table outside of Ben's door. Either Chuck or I would collect the solutions, bring them into the room, and prepare for the routine of mouth care. It was so satisfying to see Ben rinse thoroughly and then spit. It seemed to me that millions of germs were being killed off every time he rinsed. It was also a relief to have Ben cooperate, even though the solutions made his mouth sting when making contact with the mucositis.

Chuck and I developed a perfect rotation system. If I stayed the night, Chuck would arrive at the hospital around 4:00 p.m. We would all visit together until about 6:00 p.m. At that time, I would leave, and it would be Chuck's turn to stay. Chuck did not arrive until that late afternoon hour because he worked at the apartment. We had a computer and fax connected to our clinic in Florida so that Chuck could follow the operations of the business every day.

During the two hours when we were both in Ben's room, we were extra careful to not get in the way of any staff person who might need to work in the small space. Since our room was our safety zone from germs, the only people allowed in were the nurses, doctors, a nursing assistant, and one cleaning lady. The room was cleaned every single day with a mop that was designated for Ben's room only. There was a closet located on the unit that had sixteen different mop heads hanging on hooks. The cleaning lady also had special sprays and cloths for each individual room. This separation of supplies was another system to protect the children from the spread of germs. Never could a mop be used in one child's room and then taken into another child's room. Every patient had a separate set of cleaning supplies, and we were again pleased with the strict rule.

When it was time for Ben's meal tray to be delivered, it was left outside on the often-visited fold-down table. The tray was always covered with a plastic top, and each food item inside was individually wrapped with plastic wrap. The food was hot and fresh. Even with the hospital's food, Ben had only thirty minutes to eat what looked good to him. It was important to watch the clock because after thirty minutes, the tray with any leftover food had to be removed from the room. In fact, the parents were encouraged to get the tray entirely off the unit, and a cart was located in the anteroom for convenience. It was too risky that the exposed food might begin to develop organisms that could hurt Ben or the other children. Although the rules and the system were new to us, we were catching on quickly.

It was my turn to go home that night, so when our visit ended and the sun began to set, I gathered the book I was trying to read, my glasses, contact holder, pen, notebook, and sweatshirt. Chuck handed me the apartment key, so I was physically ready to leave.

I kissed Chuck on the lips and Ben on the forehead.

Ben fussed. "Don't go, Mommy. Just stay."

"I have to go home, honey, I have to take a shower and see Dana. I will give her a big hug and kiss for you," I promised.

He stretched out his arms toward me and said, "No, Mommy, just stay."

After another hug and kiss, he finally was satisfied that the shift change was fine and that it would be good to spend time with his daddy.

As I walked out of the room, I prayed for Ben's little body and his life. Frankly, I was afraid to leave my baby's side because I did not know if he would still be alive when I returned. We had forced his body into a state of extreme vulnerability. Without an immune system, he was unable to defend himself in any way. Only God could protect him now, so I prayed.

July 4, 2001 Day -1

I spent the day with Ben so Chuck could go home, take a nap, see Dana, and shower. I read Ben two books, and together we watched three movies. The rest of the day was spent napping.

Although it should have been my turn to stay the night, Chuck offered to return to the hospital after dinner to pull a "double" because I was very tired. I accepted the opportunity to spend two nights in a row back at the apartment. Even though I did not tell Chuck this, I had a plan brewing that needed me to be free to work out the details.

When I finally arrived home, I played with Dana, gave her a bath, and put her to bed. I then sat in bed and watched a parade and some fireworks on a local television channel. My eyes saw the broadcast display of pyrotechnics, but my thoughts were focused only on tomorrow's transplant.

The day for which we had prepared so long and hard was finally upon us.

25

Transplant Day

July 5, 2001 Day 0

Transplant Day!!! This was the day for which we had been waiting for so long, and I wanted it to be unforgettably special. Miss Patty, her daughter Lisa, and Dana worked at the apartment while I went to town and bought a dozen brightly colored balloons from the floral department of the grocery store. Although I was alone in the car with all of the helium-filled balloons, I soon found myself laughing out loud as if I were riding with a busload of fun friends. I sensed how hilarious I must have looked as I tried to drive back to the apartment with the balloons floating wildly all over the inside of the car. I gave a short prayer of thanks to God for all of His gifts as I continued on my way home.

This joy started the day off right. The anticipation of the re-infusion of the healthy cells was growing minute by minute inside me. I absolutely couldn't wait to get the cells back into Ben. I was more than ready for the "rescue," as the doctor called it. I had a nervous excitement whizzing through me, and I was full of positive energy. My whole being was focused on having this transplant succeed. Today was truly the first day of the rest of our lives.

The balloons were going to be a big surprise for Ben and Chuck. Patty and I tied a strip of paper to the end of each balloon's long string. On each strip of paper was typed the prayer, "Thank you, Jesus, for healing three-year-old Ben of cancer!"

To add to our surprise, we were going to play a special song for Ben. Miss Patty, while shopping one day, found a cassette tape called *Kidselebration: Personalized Name Tunes*. It was recorded and distributed by a company called Monogram International and written by Mr. Michael Rosenbaum back in 1986, long before Ben was even a thought, but it was surely written just for him. The first song on the tape was the name song, "Benjamin." The words of the song were perfect for our occasion:

> "Hello, Benjamin, how do you do?
> I'm gonna sing some songs for you.
> Some fast songs, some slow songs,
> Funny songs, too,
> So join in and sing along
> And have some fun, too!
> We're gonna sing about Benjamin,
> A very special boy.
> When he gets up in the morning,
> Until he sleeps in the evening,
> It's a special world for Benjamin
> 'Cause he's a special boy!
> So clap your hands for Benjamin and his special world.
> Every day's a new beginning,
> A chance for taking and for giving.
> So raise your voice and start singing for this special boy.
> So raise your voice and start singing for this special boy!"

Lisa made a giant poster that read, "Ben's Hoo-Ray Day," so we brought that to the hospital, too. Lisa is a talented young teenager, and her artwork goes far beyond her years. I smiled with thanks when she showed me the poster. It was terrific.

The plan was to have a party, a transplant party. The four of us arrived at the hospital at 10:30 a.m. We scrubbed extra long and hard in the anteroom while each of us took a turn holding onto the balloons so that they would not float up into the special ventilation ducts on the ceiling. Dana sat patiently in her stroller until it was her turn to be held up to the sink. She was giggling and talking her baby talk to the many colors circling around her head. Each of us was celebrating openly. This was a huge day, and we were not going to let it pass by silently.

The head nurse responded to our call to the anteroom almost immediately. Before Dana could enter the unit, she first had to have a brief physical examination, and we had to answer a series of questions about any recent exposures she might have had. This was a familiar routine. Once per week this had to be done in order for Dana to be permitted anywhere near Ben.

No siblings were allowed to wander around the unit. If a sibling was approved after an exam, he or she was allowed to go from the anteroom directly to the patient's room and inside. That was it. They were not allowed to linger in the hallway for even a few seconds, and they were not allowed in the parent room. The medical staff took no chances, and the risk of siblings, especially the little kids, infecting the floor was not a risk that anyone was willing to take. It was another strict rule that was sometimes difficult to understand, but a rule, nonetheless, that we grew to appreciate.

I felt very sorry for our neighbor, however, because he was an eight-year-old boy who was especially close to his twelve-year-old sister. Throughout his treatment for leukemia, he drew his strength from his loving sister. She had become his anchor, yet now during the most critical part of his program, she was not allowed to be on the floor with him. Her parents had to fight long and hard for their daughter to be allowed into his room for extended periods of time, and finally they won their battle. I was secretly overjoyed for them. They needed each other, and they were the perfect example of brotherly and sisterly love. I grew to love this family very much and prayed for them almost as much as I prayed for Ben. There were days when I asked God to work miracles in every single child on that floor because what I was witnessing needed more than human medical efforts— these children needed supernatural intervention.

Dana passed her examination as expected, so we were ready to move on with our grand event.

When the new, clean cells arrived in the six-pack-sized tote cooler, the nurse announced that she would be right in to get started. All of us, except Ben, had donned masks, so all that we could see of each other were our eyes. We could tell, though, that each of us had a contagious smile beneath our masks.

When Ben saw the balloons, he sat up. With a blushing grin on his face, he gave us one of his shy "howdy" waves. If I could have read his mind, I would have guessed him to be thinking something like, "So, what are they up to now?" The nurse, also suited in protective garments, finally came in.

It was exactly 11:00 a.m. As the nurse carefully held the bag of new cells in her hand, she announced, "This is it!"

A Test of Faith

Miss Patty pressed "play" on the tape recorder, and the party began. We sang out loud, we danced, we raised our arms, and we laughed at each other. Dana was in Chuck's arms, and he spun around and around with her as we all listened to her belly laugh. Ben was going crazy with happiness as we sang his name song loudly and with great passion. His arms waved in the air, and his eyes beamed with intense joy. He laughed and clapped his hands as we celebrated his life.

When the song finished, the next part of our plan began. The nurse needed to go through her checklist to prepare for the infusion of the cells, so she was busy at one corner of the room getting her equipment ready. Chuck was instructed by me to hold Ben in his arms and take him over to the window to be able to see down into the courtyard garden.

Miss Patty, Lisa, Dana, and I then took off, and as quickly as we could, we went down the five floors via the elevator and out the side door of the hospital closest to the courtyard. The balloons in tow were getting tangled because they were vigorously blowing around in the wind that we were creating by running. The people in the lobby just stared, and I'm sure a thousand questions passed through their minds. We laughed and Dana clapped as Lisa pushed her stroller at maximum speed. The wheels of her portable umbrella stroller were dancing as they could hardly manage to keep up with our pace.

In the courtyard, we looked up and searched for Ben's window. Finally, we saw his little arm waving at us, so it was time. We released the balloons and watched as they slowly began to float up towards the cloudless, blue sky. After just a few seconds, the balloons floated right past Ben's window. They were so close that if no windowpane was there, he probably could have reached out and touched them. We cheered, jumped up and down, danced in circles again, and cried. I hugged Dana and then Miss Patty and Lisa. I pumped both of my arms into the clean air, and I shouted, "WAY TO GO, BEN!"

Closing my eyes, I whispered to God and to my mom to please send angels, and I smiled. I'm sure that anyone watching thought that we truly had lost our minds. In a way we had. We were beyond the point of exhilaration. We had just released twelve balloons, each with a declaration of Jesus' promise to us. We proclaimed and accepted the victory, and we wanted the world to know it. We knew that we were trusting in God and that He was with Benjamin. We knew that life was great. To this day, I often wonder where those balloons ended up and who may have read the tags. I hope someone who needed to know of God's great grace and salvation had the opportunity to pick up one of our messages.

Several people were sitting on the benches having an early lunch when the balloons were released. They asked questions, and we shared our story. They cheered with us and offered congratulations and many smiles. I was beaming.

The nurse waited for us to return to the room, which, of course, required the usual scrub time. After we were finally cleaned up, we again joined Ben and Chuck and the nurse. When we entered the room, Ben was back in bed but still sitting. He was quiet but said thanks with the biggest smile I had ever seen on his face. Chuck came over and hugged me, and I noticed that he was crying. The nurse was, too. She said in seventeen years of working on transplant units, she had never seen such a celebration, and she loved it.

I found out later that when we were running downstairs, our nurse told the other nurses what was going on, and they in turn told their patients. The patients who were able went to their windows with their parents and watched the balloons pass by. The whole floor was celebrating with us, and it was fantastic.

At 11:17 a.m., the new cells began dripping into Ben, and by 11:24 a.m., he began to experience a severe and violent reaction to them. The sudden change in emotion came like the strike of a lightning bolt. It was so unexpected and fierce that we were all taken aback. His reaction to the cells started with severe itching. A rash began to spread on his bald head and pale cheeks. It rapidly progressed before our eyes into large hives and welts all over his head, neck, and face. Soon his entire face was flushed, and the red, bumpy welts began to move down to his neck, chest, abdomen, and legs. His temperature rose as if the thermometer was being placed in a pot of boiling water. He was yelling that his feet hurt, so I tried to rub them.

I prayed, "What's happening, Lord? Please, God, help us! Please save Ben. We need your help, Father."

The hives were moving down Ben's body like the water of a flood gushing over the banks of a river out onto the street. He was irritable and crying and sweating, and he was quickly beginning to panic. We

A Test of Faith

all were, even the nurse. She pushed an emergency button, which alerted the doctor, who was on the floor. At all times, a physician was on the unit. There was never a minute that one was not immediately available because of the grave situations that could develop so suddenly…like this one.

The attending physician raced in, still rubbing in the foam he had squirted onto his hands. I was amazed that he remembered to use the cleanser but realized that this was strict protocol, and as such, it had to be done before entering anyone's room, for any reason.

The doctor brought several syringes with him. When he looked at Ben, he immediately put one of the syringes onto the pump and began a rapid administration. Miss Patty held Dana close to her chest as they stood as far back into a corner as they could. Lisa stood close to her mom with her arms wrapped tightly around her mother's elbow. Chuck and I hovered as close to Ben's bed as possible.

"What's happening?" Chuck asked.

The doctor did not answer. He loaded a second syringe to a second pump, which had been attached to the IV pole earlier in the day. The contents of that syringe immediately began to pour into Ben's garden hose, joining the medicines already there.

When Ben finally stopped crying and reported that the itching was going away, we all breathed a massive sigh of relief. I turned to look at Miss Patty, who was trying to wipe the tears that were pouring down her cheeks. She smiled, but it was forced. She had fallen in love with our family and was now a part of it. We loved her, too, like one of our own. We were together, and we were doing our best as a family.

It took two hours to stabilize Ben. When he was finally comfortable, he fell fast asleep. The doctor explained what had happened.

"It appears to me that Ben has had a systemic reaction to the steroids that we gave him in preparation for this infusion," he said in a calm voice.

In preparing for a potential rejection, the medical staff had learned that steroids must be given to the patient to reduce the risk of any problems when giving back the stem cells. The doctor thought that this significant reaction was probably more in response to the steroids than to the clean cells.

The doctor's explanation made little sense to me. I don't know what happened that morning, but I believe Ben had an allergic reaction to one of the chemicals used to preserve the cells because the reaction was so sudden and so specific to the time when the cells started entering his body. Regardless of the cause, I was relieved that it was over.

Ben's color returned to normal, and the welts dissipated. He no longer itched, and his temperature returned to normal. Soon he was resting comfortably, so I took his fire-truck blanket from the end of the bed and tucked it gently under his chin. I kissed him long and hard on his cheek and then wiped away the tear that had fallen onto his head. I backed away, grabbed a towel, and cried hard, muffling my sobs.

Ben recovered without incident. Most of the afternoon following the transplant, he slept. A member of the medical team came in to check on him and recorded his vital signs every fifteen minutes.

Miss Patty, Dana, and Lisa went back to the apartment while Chuck and I stayed with Ben. Chuck tried to read a men's fitness magazine and I tried to read a book, but neither of us could concentrate. Instead, we found ourselves watching every breath that Ben took. I clutched the nurse's call button in my hand.

I can't remember who went home that night. All I remember is that we were both there at Ben's side until it was very late.

26

Grow Cells Grow

> July 6, 2001 DAY +1

"GROW CELLS GROW!" This motto on the floor of the transplant unit was well known and worshipped by everyone, and it was now our prayer. Ben's white blood cell count had dropped to zero, as expected. The new cells had been infused, so now it was time to wait for these new cells to grow. We were told that it could take as few as fifteen days for the cells to engraft, or as long as forever.

Sometimes the new cells just did not have the ability to find their way into the proper place in the body where they could have the opportunity to multiply and reproduce a new immune system. I did not ask what would happen if Ben's transplant didn't work because I instinctively knew the answer: Ben would die. It made sense that another bag of cells could be infused, and I was thankful that we still had one bag left in storage. A second transplant could be attempted with hopes that Ben's body would accept the cells. If it still didn't, however, he would not have any ability to defend against infection because the immune system that he once had would be gone forever.

The happy, positive, outgoing traits of Ben's personality had prevailed through all of the rough times so far. Even when he felt awful, he took it in stride. On occasion, he would still surprise me with a request to go for a wagon ride or watch a movie, or he would talk or tell one of his favorite stories. He usually gave a "thumbs up" sign when the doctor asked how he was doing, and the thumbs up would be accompanied by a heartwarming, lovable smile. Most of the days throughout the course of this lengthy protocol, Ben had given a "double thumbs up" signal for the day. He was good at making the gesture. He was always bold, strong, and affirming when he put out his closed fist with a straight, extended thumb. Today was different, though.

Ben, like all babies, offered many smiles right after birth. Most of these smiles were more related to gas than a true expression of a happy emotion. When he did begin to smile voluntarily, however, he did it often. But today, I saw something different. For the very first time in his life, not once during this day did he smile. Not once did he look at anything with favor. In fact, he felt so miserable that he could not speak at all; he could only pull his hand out from under the blanket to give a "thumbs down" sign. I did not know that he knew how to gesture this negative sentiment, but somehow I was glad that he did. I was surprised with all he had been through that a thumb's down had not come at least once before this. After all, he was entitled to feel lousy.

Ben was in pretty bad shape physically, but I think he had hit an emotional low, too. He could not sit up. He would not eat or drink, and he did not have the energy to be a part of any conversation. I didn't force him. He needed time to be left alone, sleep, rest, and get better. The good guy cells had to have a chance to set up shop and start growing, and they did not need to be bothered. I continued to pray over and over again, "Please Lord, help his cells to grow."

July 7, 2001 DAY +2

Our most important job of all at this point was to keep Ben completely free from any exposure to germs. Our most prominent risk was that of pneumonia or other respiratory invasion. I had already seen several of the children transferred to the pediatric intensive care unit, and sadly, several of these children never had the opportunity to return to the unit. Their precious lives were abruptly snatched away because of a lung infection.

I asked the cleaning lady to wear not only a mask, but a gown, too. In addition, I cleaned the room myself several times a day with rubbing alcohol. I wiped down the floor, countertop, doorknobs, handrails on the bed, computer equipment, and even the windowsill. I cleaned everything. I'm not sure if it was obsessive behavior, but it kept me busy and made me feel as if I was doing everything in my power to keep the room safe for Ben's depleted body.

When Ben had his eyes open, I shared my cleaning energy with him. I soaked two washcloths with the rubbing alcohol and put one under each of my feet. I glided around the room as if I was wearing ice skates, and on several occasions, I acted like a clown and pretended that I was falling down on the ice. Sometimes I thought Ben was really enjoying my ludicrous behavior, so I went on with the little skit. On other occasions, he just slowly opened his eyes, looked at me, and then closed his eyes again.

I wasn't taking anything personally during these days. If he didn't want any part of my witless sense of humor, that was ok with me. On the many previous occasions that I had preformed, he loved it and laughed at me. I knew that he liked the comedy routine, so it was there for him when he was good and ready for it. Today was not the day. Today's white blood cell count was still zero.

July 8, 2001 DAY +3

They started Ben on the TPN feeding on this third day after the transplant. Another pump was added to the IV pole, which made the total number of pumps now three. These pumps managed the twenty-four-hour, intravenous feeding system, as well as all of the medications and fluids required to keep his body at a safe homeostatic level. He had not eaten for a few days, but, more importantly, he had not had anything to drink, so it was time to give him some nourishment artificially.

Each day, no matter how bad Ben felt, he had to be forced out of bed to stand on a scale so that the doctors could have an idea about his fluid and nourishment status. Like most of the children at this stage, Ben began to quickly lose weight, so intervention was immediately given before he became dangerously dehydrated.

Up until this day, Ben could at least be lifted to the scale where he could independently stand for the few seconds required for the computer to register his weight. Today, however, I had to weigh myself first and then hold Ben in my arms and do the math to calculate his weight. Because of his lack of strength, he was not at all able to stand alone. His little legs were completely atrophied to the point where he had virtually no muscle definition in his calves or thighs, and the energy in his body was completely gone. He could not even sit up to the side of the bed by himself. One of us had to lift him. The sight was pitiful.

Sandie Klassen

I noticed when I was on the scale that I had already lost eleven pounds myself. I knew I had to force myself to eat and drink because I needed to maintain my health and strength to be able to care for Ben, but nothing was appealing. I knew that if I got sick, I would be banned from the unit and from seeing Ben, which was something I most certainly could not have handled emotionally. I had seen what had happened when one mother was asked to leave the unit because she was so run down that she could hardly stand. As she was leaving, she was nothing short of hysterical. I felt so incredibly sorry for her, and the event shook my stability. She definitely forced me to turn my attention a little more to my personal health responsibilities.

I tried to stay focused in the hospital and worked hard to keep Ben safe from infection. I tried to force him to do his mouth care, but it was impossible. He just moaned and pulled away. He was also supposed to have a bath every day, but there was no way in the world to manage it. The boy did not have the strength or ability to keep his eyes open, let alone be able to endure the rigors of standing or even sitting for a bath. Enough was enough.

Everything, including routine activities of daily living, took extraordinary internal motivation to accomplish during this time because to me, nothing seemed significant or worth any energy. I had to force myself to eat, make the bed, clean the apartment, and pay the bills. I thanked God for Miss Patty every day. She truly helped us to survive.

July 9, 2001 DAY +4

Four days after transplant, Ben's white blood count was still zero. He required a blood transfusion and some platelets because those counts had once again dropped to dangerously low levels. His body was not working at all to build blood independently, and he needed some assistance. He also needed help for some routine processes, such as vomiting, urinating, and even breathing. He was on a low flow of oxygen to help make respiration and blood oxygenation easier for him. He needed assistance from every direction on these early days after the transplant, and I had to face the fact that he simply needed assistance just to stay alive.

A Test of Faith

He needed me, too. As much as I wanted to crawl into a ball and turn my face from the realities of the day, I knew that more than anything in the world right now, Ben needed Chuck and me to stay strong, stay alert, and stay at his side directing the way. Even if he were a grown man, he still would have required the capable mind and body of someone else to watch over him at this point. Adults going through bone marrow transplants, like children, also need the confidence of someone who loves them to get them past this critical time. They, too, need someone to watch over the medicines being administered, the examinations being performed, and the discussions being held.

Ben continued to throw up, but his body had absolutely no strength to perform the action. He had to be helped to a sitting position so that he could slump forward and place his head into his bucket. I placed one hand on his back and held the bucket securely with my other hand. I stayed in this position for six hours straight.

The painful, wrenching vomiting soon turned to nothing but dry heaves. By late afternoon, he was still heaving, and I noticed that the corner of his right eye was filled with bright red blood. At first I panicked, but then I realized that he had simply broken a blood vessel from the repeated attempts to vomit.

The mouth sores were growing more complicated and numerous, but Ben had yet to be put on any pain medicine. I was beginning to wonder why. I was feeling beyond helpless. There was nothing to do but wait, clean his room, and pray, so I prayed fervently and frequently. "Please, dear God, let these cells grow and grow. Come on, Jesus, now is the time. Let's do it! Please, hear our prayer, Lord." The only other thing I could do was to focus on Ben and his blood counts.

July 10, 2001 DAY +5

I had never seen such an intense fear and helplessness in another person's eyes as I saw when my eyes met Ben's on this day. He looked at me and pleaded for help. He spoke not a word, but I could see and hear his thoughts. I felt empty and vulnerable. I completely lacked any power to help him. I spent a lot of time reading my Bible. I wanted to trust God and to push away all of my doubts, but the doubts were there, gnawing at me. I was not sure if Ben could survive this.

Many times before this day, I had wanted to change places with Ben, but now, more desperately than ever before, I would have done anything to be the one with cancer. I wanted nothing more than for me to be the one sick in bed, and my little boy to be the perfectly healthy one at my side. I was so incredibly mad that I wanted to scream and protest to the world and to the almighty creator Himself that allowing a child to go through with this was not only unfair, it certainly was nothing less than wicked.

My roller coaster of emotions had traveled at terrific speeds to take me from defeat and despair to anger and hostility. I gritted my teeth as I wiped away the ceaseless flow of tears, but remarkably, at the same time, I wanted to praise God. This tremendous depth of illness that we were experiencing was exactly what the doctors had hoped to see. Although I was angry with God, I was finding within me the ability to give Him thanks because the transplant was working. The doctors had confidence that their little patient would once again grow strong and healthy and that this was simply a stage that we had to go through before we could get better. The doctors and the nurses agreed that this type of severe reaction meant that we could be very certain that Ben's entire bone marrow was wiped out, and nothing could be better from the perspective of curing the cancer.

"It'll just take time," they said. "We usually expect ten to twenty-one days at this stage, so hang in there. You have to be strong for your baby."

Ten to twenty-one days. I thought they were out of their minds. Just the thought of watching Ben lie there for one more day seemed impossible.

The pain from the mucositis was growing more and more intense for Ben, so a fourth pump was added to the IV pole, and a continuous drip of morphine was connected to his garden hose. The mucositis was horrendous. When the doctor asked Ben to open his mouth for the day's examination, he shined a flashlight into a mouth that looked as if it were full of white cotton balls. Ben moaned in pain while trying to keep his mouth open long enough to satisfy the doctor, whom he always wanted to please.

His fever was up to 103.6, but that did not seem to concern anyone accept us. After all, the girl down the hall had a fever of

A Test of Faith

106.1. I did not sleep again that night, but rather kept putting cool cloths onto Ben's forehead. I soaked the washcloth in a cup of sterile ice water, rang it out until it was damp only, and then I placed it onto Ben's fire-hot forehead. I had made ice cubes from a sterile bottle of water several days earlier in case Ben wanted an ice cube in his drink. I had hoped that a cold ice cube or beverage would soothe his painful mouth, but he never wanted one. I added these pre-made cubes and sterile water to a cup, and this became the source of my cold water for his feverish head. I stroked his legs with my cool hands and prayed. The doctors reassured us that this high fever was normal and that Ben was doing well.

"How can you say that?" I wondered but didn't ask aloud. "He can't lift his head off of the pillow, he can't open his eyes, and he can't speak, so how can you say he's doing well?"

I knew deep down that I had to trust their judgment. We had brought Ben to Duke because it was the best place in the world for our son. If this was all to be expected, I had to accept it and be strong all the way through it.

July 11, 2001 DAY +6

As a precautionary measure, the doctor ordered studies of Ben's blood because of the high fever. All of his cultures came back negative, so the fever was just as everyone had initially expected—a result of the body's effort in trying to get the white cells to grow. Much to our dismay, however, the morning's studies revealed that the white blood count was still zero.

Miss Patty asked nearly every minute of every day what she could do to help us. She was beginning to see the fatigue in our bodies and the lost of zest in our eyes, and she, too, was feeling useless. When neither Chuck nor I could give a concrete answer as to what might help, Miss Patty took matters into her own hands. She and Dana went to the library and rented some movies about fire trucks. She called and asked if she could help by coming to the hospital to stay at Ben's side for awhile so that Chuck, Dana, and I could get something to eat and some fresh air. She then told me about the movies she had worked hard to clean over the past hour so that they could be brought onto the unit. She finally had them in the condition they needed to be in to pass our germ test, including packing them in the Ziploc bag, and she wanted to bring them to Ben. She said that she also felt that Chuck and I needed some time alone together, so she sort of insisted that I take her up on the offer.

I hesitated on the phone as I thought things over. I did need a break, and I desperately needed to be with Dana and Chuck. After a few seconds, I agreed.

Patty sounded relieved and happy on the other end of the line. She said that she would be at the hospital within thirty minutes.

After I hung up the phone, I looked over at Ben, who was sound asleep. Drool oozed from the corner of his mouth, and I could hear a little gurgling sound as he breathed in his heavy, deep-sleep rhythm. I wiped the drool, kissed his forehead, and then sat down to put on my shoes.

Miss Patty came to the hospital late in the morning and was ready to spend the entire day at Ben's side. She had Dana dressed in a beautiful, white eyelet dress with a red ribbon running through it and white, open-toed sandals. When I went into the anteroom to meet them, I hurried to Dana for a big bear hug. She was standing without holding on to anyone and looked so proud of herself. She had recently taken her very first steps and was quickly changing and growing from a tiny baby into a little girl. She pointed to the door and said, "Ben, Ben," but the nurses could not let her anywhere near him these days. Even though she was in perfect health and had no risky exposures to other children, Ben's state was too weak to allow for any toddler visits.

Miss Patty stayed with Ben while Chuck, Dana, and I walked all over the beautiful Duke University campus. We pushed Dana in the stroller until we came to the mid-quad section of the west campus, right in front of the chapel. At that point, Dana was let out of the stroller so that she could run between us on the plush, soft, summer grass. The focal point of the entire university, the chapel, rose up brilliantly before us. The gothic architecture made us think that it was an old European cathedral built in the 1700s or earlier, when, in fact, it was not completed until 1930. The stained-glass windows and carvings of Biblical figures were magnificent. It was a welcome sight, so peaceful and spirit filled.

The three of us had lunch, talked, rolled in the grass, walked through the Sarah Duke Gardens, ate ice cream, and bought some

A Test of Faith

Duke shirts, hats, and banners at the college bookstore. Our day was truly peaceful and happy. It was alive, it was healthy, and it was full of hope. It was the best day I had had in a long time, and it inspired me to be strong during our trials. Dana talked her gibberish and did a lot of pointing, so I think she had fun, too. She needed this time with us as much as we needed it with her.

When we finally returned to Ben's room, the sun had set and the summer air was cool and fresh. As much as I wanted to see Ben again and be at his side, the thought of going back into that isolated room and being surrounded by medicine and illness was taking everything out of me. I had to go, I knew, but what I wanted more was to have Ben with us out in the world, free from worries, hospitals, and sickness.

I left Chuck and Dana in the anteroom and went to Ben's room. Miss Patty was sitting on the tiny blue stool when I peeked through the open blind on the door's window. She was right next to Ben, and she had her hands folded with her forehead resting on top of them. At first, I thought maybe she was asleep, so I was as quiet as I could be.

Patty looked up immediately when I opened the door. I was still rubbing the large dollop of foam soap between my fingers and up to my elbows as I looked over at Ben, who was still asleep in the same position in which I had left him several hours earlier.

Patty and I whispered as we shared the stories of our day. She said that Ben did great and that he was awake for quite some time after we left. He loved the fire truck movie and stayed awake for almost all of it. She helped prop him up on pillows so that he could watch, and he concentrated and showed quite a bit of interest. She said he even wanted to hold her hand so that they could watch the fire trucks together.

Miss Patty was glowing. The time she had spent with Ben was bonding and so rejuvenating for both of them. It was great for Ben to have her with him because he loved her and missed her so much. He wanted to do things for her that he would not consider doing for anyone else in the world. He was madly in love with his nanny. Their relationship was special, and so was their day together. Miss Patty is such a wonderful person to all of us. She is beautiful inside and out, and she holds a very important place in each of our hearts. She is truly our angel.

Later that evening, after Patty, Chuck, and Dana had gone home, I told Ben about our day and how silly Dana was when she was walking and rolling in the grass. I didn't think he was listening to me because his eyes were closed, and he made no facial expression to acknowledge any of my words. As I turned away from him to sit back down in my chair, from the corner of my eye I saw his arm move. When I turned back toward him, he was looking at me, and he was smiling. It was a very weak smile, but it said so much.

He was still with us.

27

Just Keep Waiting

July 12, 2001 DAY +7

Ben was very sick. The mucositis was beyond belief. The discomfort Ben was experiencing was so fierce that he could not sleep for more than twenty minutes at a time, around the clock, without having to scream out in pain. His screams were muffled and strained because his throat and mouth hurt too much to push any sound through them.

The doctor ordered the morphine pump to be turned up several notches to help give our boy some relief, but even that did not seem to help. I tried everything I could think of to help my son, but there simply was nothing I could do that made any difference to the misery he was experiencing. Every few minutes, I walked to his bedside and pushed the morphine pump button for him. I was not really supposed to do this because the design of the pain pump was such that it was "patient independent," but I felt it was the least I could do to help Ben. He did not have the strength to push the small red button that loosely lay in his little fisted hand.

Ben was so weak that he actually fell asleep with his head in the vomit pail. He did not have the energy to hold his head up, but he refused to lie back down in his bed.

The fevers continued to register between 100 and 102.7. I could only trust that the cells were doing something deep in his body. I could only trust that they were searching for a secure place where they could begin to reproduce, grow, and function. The books and the doctors said that fevers often prefaced some sort of white count, so I was hopeful and wishful and prayerful that this elevation in body temperature meant that something good was happening.

I felt completely helpless by this point. I was doing all that I could to keep from falling apart. Nothing could snap me out of my depression. I couldn't figure out why I was feeling this way, and I was struggling with the emotion. There was absolutely nothing I could do to facilitate the process of cell growth; the only way I could help Ben was to stay at his side and pray for him.

> July 13, 2001 DAY +8

Because of the mouth and digestive tract sores, Ben could no longer speak, swallow, or breathe through his mouth. The air passing over the sores was much too painful for him, and the idea of swallowing even naturally produced saliva was impossible.

He rested with his head on his pillow and let the drool seep out of the corner of his mouth. The saliva was mixed with bright blood, and it was the most horrific and frightful sight that I had seen yet. I could hardly bear to watch him drool, but I had no choice. I gently wiped the corner of his mouth every few minutes with a cool, wet cloth.

I worried constantly because I had not seen my son open his eyes for a few days now. I wondered, "If my God is so loving, how could he let this child go through this much only to let him die?" Ben just lay in his bed moaning. He could not speak or even move. I asked him once to lift his arm so that I could untangle his hoses, but he could not do it. His body was virtually comatose, and I was beyond feeling crippled with helplessness.

"Please, Lord, I'm trusting you," I prayed out loud. My voice was hoarse.

I tried ever so gently to change Ben's diaper, but that, too, was incredibly painful for him. The diaper rash on his buttocks was getting worse every minute, and small blisters had started to form. His anus was inflamed and swollen from the mucositis that was growing and invading his entire digestive tract from inside to outside. The wet, cool washcloths were not helping to relieve the pain. The texture of the soft washcloth was too much for his raw skin to tolerate, but I had to do something to keep the area clean from potential germ-infesting feces.

I buzzed the nurse to ask for some help. I could not bear to see Ben whimpering and wincing in pain over what I had to do to him. The nurse soon answered my call and entered the room with a rather large tub of Duke's special "Colonel's Cream." One of the staff members had concocted this thick, white zinc cream several years ago, and it was approved for use on the unit. The cream was like a smooth, odorless paste. The nurse who helped to develop this blend of soothing and healing agents also could not bear to see what these children were going through, so she spent hours trying to help by creating this magical cream.

It worked magnificently to calm down the rash within hours. Ben winced in pain when I tried to apply the cream, but I felt I had to continue with its use over the weeks because I could see how wonderfully it was working to soothe the sensitive tissue. As painful as the task was for both of us, I knew deep down that I had to continue with my efforts to help. I worked as gently as I could, but I know I still hurt him. It tore me up to have to do it.

As lost and weak minded as I had become, I had to continue to have total faith that God had a great future planned for this boy. After all, he was such a special child, full of energy and life. He had already touched so many lives, and he had so much potential to continue to do so.

July 14, 2001 DAY +9

Chuck and I were doing our best to keep any germ, fungus, virus, bacteria, or infection away from our little room on the ward and away from our precious miracle, our son. I spent the majority of my time wiping down everything in the room with rubbing alcohol. My industrial-size, half-gallon bottle was now only about half full, and the germs were dead. Ben had stayed safe from infection so far, so either the alcohol, the prayers, or both were working.

"Please cells, grow already!" was all I could think about.

July 15, 2001 DAY +10

We continued to wait and tried to be patient, but the reports were still the same: no cell growth.

Finally, however, there was evidence that something different was happening in Ben's little body. He was still lingering in what I called a "semi-comatose" state, but he was now beginning to show signs of agitation and anger. You should be, I thought. I would be furious if I were you. I would be mad at the entire world if they beat me up as badly as we all have done to you.

So, the good news was that he got mad at me and tried to act on it. I was standing next to his bed, just watching him. He opened his eyes, looked right at me, and then tried to push me away. He flung his small fist at me, grunted with vigilance, and rolled onto his side to face away from me. I was stunned because I was not touching him, talking to him, or anything. I was just standing there. I was glad to take the hit. He needed to express himself; it was good for his recovery. His moment of anger showed that he was still fighting hard inside, and that was all that mattered.

About four hours into the afternoon, I was trying to straighten out Ben's blankets when he started to yell at me. "Get away from me! Leave me alone! Go away!" he tried to shout. His voice was fairly strong, and he produced a coherent sound rather than the grunt to which I was becoming accustomed. He was pronouncing words that I could clearly hear! I was shocked at first to hear him talk to me like that, but then, to myself, I smiled.

My smile faded quickly when I realized how insulted I was by his words. Furthermore, my feelings were badly hurt. Rationally, I knew that I could not take his words personally. I knew that he did not mean what he said. However, I wanted to help him more than anything in the entire world, and I was so fragile that his anger at me was hurtful. I had to force myself not to cry or yell back at him.

Still feeling stunned, I sat down in the chair. I wanted to go away and leave him alone, just as he had demanded.

Within minutes of his aggressive outburst of anger, Ben opened his eyes. He looked at me and just started crying. I got up out of my chair and walked over to him to determine if what I was seeing was for real. It was. Ben was crying, and the tears were falling down his cheeks right onto his pillow. I gently picked him up and held him tightly in my arms for a long, long time. I did not speak a word. I just held him as I sat on the edge of his bed.

It felt so good to hold my baby. We could barely move because of all of the tubes and junk hooked up to him, but we sat there together. It was the first time in days that he had let me touch him, let alone hold him. His heart was pounding against mine, and his face was burrowed in the crux of my neck. He breathed heavily. His breath was warm on my neck as it slowed and became more rhythmical. He

A Test of Faith

calmed down and rested peacefully in my arms. I held him tightly as I kissed his head and shoulder. He never knew that I was crying, too.

> July 16, 2001 DAY +11

A child down the hall passed away this morning. The doctor came into our room to ask if he could speak to me for a minute in the hall. My heart raced as I followed him out the door. I was petrified that he had some bad news about Ben's recovery, and I was not sure if I had the strength to take it. "Oh, God," I prayed, "everything is ok, right? Please, Jesus." These were the words I spoke to my Lord as I followed the doctor out into the hallway.

The doctor had to report the news of our neighbor because there was going to be administrative work performed that we might see, such as the removal of a dead boy. Also, it was unit policy to tell all of the parents of tragedies like these because we were a close group. The social workers had set the policy many years earlier after they had attended seminars on grief. They felt that each parent should know about a death so that they could respond in the way they needed to deal with it.

I was not sure how I felt about the policy. I understood perfectly how close we all were, though. Sharing bathrooms and heartache, we grew to love each other's children and shared in each other's triumphs and devastations. We prayed for each other and really wished the best for each other. Although this was a family I had not yet had the opportunity to know well, the death was numbing. I felt for the grieving parents as I had never before felt for another parent. I sensed how they must have been feeling, but I was desperate to never really know.

I thanked the doctor for his time and genuine concern for our feelings. He turned to walk to the next room with the sad news, and I turned to go back into Ben's room. I had to wait a minute before I could go back into the room, so I washed with the foam hand soap twice. Slowly, too. I rubbed the soap between each finger and up my forearms to my elbows. I thanked God that everything was ok with Ben, and I prayed for peace for the family down the hall. I also asked if Jesus would please hold that precious baby tight in His arms as he went to heaven.

July 17, 2001 DAY +12

WE'VE GOT CELLS!!!!! The lab report indicated that Ben's white count was measurable at 0.2! I was so relieved, exhausted, and overjoyed. So many happy emotions flowed, and the excitement and adrenaline coursed through each and every one of my veins, but I felt too weak to express anything. This highway of ups and downs, joys and sorrows, encouragements and letdowns was taking its toll on me. When I received the news of the cells—finally, some cells—all I wanted to do was fall onto the floor flat on my face and breathe a sigh of relief. At the same time, however, I wanted to scream and yell out the fantastic news on the top of the nearest mountain. I wanted to run through the halls; I wanted to grab Ben and throw him into the air. I wanted to do a cartwheel, and I wanted to cry! So, after the doctor left the room, I walked back over to the window looking out over the garden. I put both of my hands on the window, high above my head, and rested my forehead on the glass. Then I smiled. I smiled with my entire heart and soul.

July 18, 2001 DAY +13

The white blood cell count rose to a remarkable and unbelievable 5.2 after only one day of measurable readings. The doctor, nurses, and even the chief of the unit came by to tell us that Ben was incredible. "We have never seen anything like this," they said. "He is our superstar!" were their exact words.

Even though Ben had some white cells, he was still very sick. We were all encouraged and exuberant but still saddened that Ben's body was not yet showing any relief from its anguish. As the bone marrow developed and tried to begin some sort of function, Ben's body was still suffering from the traumas to which it had recently been subjected. He was agitated, angry, frustrated, and miserably uncomfortable. I made him sit up, and, against his will, I forced him to stand alone on the scale to be weighed. He was still a very sick boy, but as far as I was concerned, things were looking up. There was a bright light beginning to shine on us once again, but we could not be fooled into letting our guard down. We had to continue our battle against infection, pneumonia, and complications of any sort, but I now had a renewed energy to fight. We had a miraculous healing going on here, and we were fighting for total victory.

Two different doctors came to our room, tapped on the door, entered, and shook their heads in glorious disbelief. Ben's improved cell count was truly miraculous. For the first time in my life, I was bold enough to express my faith in God out loud to others. Usually, I was used to being a very quiet Christian. I would keep my thoughts and experiences to myself, always pray alone, and never talk about God to others because I did not want to come across as some wacko, born-again "Jesus freak." Today, I was brave and audacious as I never had been before. I was in the midst of experiencing something spectacular and supernatural in my eyes, and I could not hold back in sharing my feelings.

As the attending doctor stood at the end of Ben's bed, I said, "Doctor, what do you think? Is this a miracle or what? Thank you for all that you've done for Ben. I think God has given you and this entire staff many gifts to help heal my son, but this truly is His work. Thank you for sharing in this miraculous healing."

The doctor just stared at me. My heart stopped. He looked at me a bit perplexed, and I honestly thought he was going to turn around and leave the room with raised eyebrows and a finger twirling at his temple. I nervously waited for the doctor's next words.

"You know, I think you are right," he said at last. "This recovery is fantastic, and Benjamin's counts are unbelievable. So, if it is answered prayer, I'm glad. I think I'll try it on a few things." And he turned and walked out of the room.

July 19, 2001 DAY +14

If all of this healing was so miraculous, then why was Ben still so sick? Maybe miracles just took time, I thought. Ben slept from 1:00 a.m. until 3:00 a.m., and that was it. The rest of the night was spent moaning, vomiting, and yelling at me. I could do nothing right for him. In the middle of the night, I sat in the wrong position. At 4:00 a.m., he wanted a movie, but I turned on the movie incorrectly and put the wrong video into the VCR in the first place. When I turned on the movie that he had requested, it was still the wrong one.

Sandie Klassen

I was pretty much losing all of my patience by morning, and the walls were rapidly closing in on me. I bit my tongue to not yell back at Ben. I was steaming inside and wanted to pull my hair out. All I could do was put up with his mood and watch the clock for Chuck's arrival. Over and over again in my mind, I said, "Please Chuck, hurry and get here. I need relief—and fast!"

When Chuck finally arrived, he walked into the room looking relaxed and smelling wonderfully clean. His eyes were bright, and he had a hearty laugh and sense of humor about him. When he said his jolly "Hello," I grunted a "Hi" back, picked up my bag, gave kisses and hugs, and whispered in Chuck's ear, "Good luck!" I told Chuck that I would call him later, and then I left. This was the worst transition of shifts that we had ever had, but I could not help it. I was at the end of my rope for the moment.

July 20, 2001 DAY +15

While Chuck was spending his time at the hospital, Miss Patty, Dana, Lisa, and I went out to a restaurant called "Fuddruckers." We ate hamburgers and a huge basket of French fries. We ordered beer and a gigantic vanilla ice cream, caramel, and chocolate dessert. We talked and talked and talked. I stretched my legs out onto the booth seat and wiggled my toes inside my shoes. I sipped on my cold beer and did not let the waiter take away the French fry basket until every bit of the potatoes had been consumed, crumbs and all. I relaxed and savored the laughs, discussion, and healthy adult company. It was an incredible evening with my baby daughter and extended family, Patty and Lisa.

I went to bed feeling good and possibly ready for my shift the next day. Possibly. I needed a good night's sleep and really another week out of that room. A good night's sleep was a good start, though, and I thought about Ben and Chuck when I put my head onto the pillow. I wondered how everything was going. Before long, I really couldn't wait to get back to the hospital to see the rest of my family. I went to sleep wanting more than anything for the four of us to be together at home. I wanted the simple things back that we had once taken for granted—things that I would never take for granted again. I wanted to have fun and to be a normal family doing normal things. That time would come soon, I hoped. I prayed, please let it come soon.

28

Pepperoni Pizza

July 21, 2001 DAY +16

We convinced Ben to go for a ride in the wagon about mid morning. He was not as excited about the proposition as we were, but he reluctantly went along with the plan anyway. We were out of our little room for over twenty minutes, and the change of scenery was more than refreshing for at least Chuck and me. Ben was wrapped in blankets, half sitting, but mostly just propped up against a pillow in the wagon. There was no question in my mind that he definitely was not smiling under his mask. The bucket was positioned at his feet, in arm's reach, should he begin to once again feel the frequent waves of nausea.

He was doing so much better, though. Really he was. He was yelling at us more and more, which I guess, in a way, was a good thing. His voice was clearer and stronger when he yelled, so that certainly had to be a good indication that we were making progress. His white blood cell count continued to rise, and the graph that I was keeping and had taped to the wall was looking surprisingly and thankfully exponential. I was feeling a sense of peace, and my patience for the whole situation was improving.

At this point, I felt as if I had just planted a seed in some rich, black soil, and I was checking every day to see my new bloom. I knew deep down that it would grow, and soon it would be a tall, beautiful planting. With Ben, too, I felt comfortable that all was going to be ok. I just had to wait for everything to happen in its own and God's good time.

> July 22, 2001 DAY +17

The mucositis was beginning to show signs of clearing. Ben could now open his mouth. His buttocks had cleared up at least eighty percent, and I was feeling better and better about his recovery.

The doctor had placed weaning orders on the morphine pump attached to Ben, and so far the process of slowing down the administration of the drug was going well. Because Ben's body was so small, the likelihood of a morphine addiction was very high, so the weaning process included taking away the potent narcotic painkiller and replacing it with some withdrawal medication, namely methadone.

The medical staff was trying to take Ben off as many of the intravenous medications as possible and change them to oral doses so that we could prepare for discharge to the apartment. Ben hated to take medicine orally, and these people were bringing it in by the truckload. I was convinced that they were really trying to torture me, not really trying to help Ben. Chuck and I had to be sure that he took each dose of each drug on time and in the right order. Because Ben hated it so much, the practice always resulted in a fight.

I was going absolutely mad trying to fulfill my pharmaceutical responsibilities as his caregiver. I tried to crush Pez candy and break open the capsule to mix the candy with the medicine. It did not work. I tried to mix the powders from within the capsules into some orange juice. It did not work. I tried bribes of toys, food, promises to leave him alone, whatever I could come up with, and nothing worked. I wanted to scream at this kid, but that sure would not work, either. The medicine was too important, and I could not face the fact that he was not going to take it. He had to take it; we did not have a choice. This medicine was going to help keep him safe from infection while we waited for his immune system to rebuild, and it was going to be part of the routine we would have to do for at least the next six months. I had to get something to work, or I would lose my mind. I even tried to talk to Ben as if he were a grown man. I tried to explain in detail why it was so imperative for him to take all of these medicines. I thought that if he understood the rationale behind the orders, he would understand the importance and, therefore, comply. That tactic did not work, either. You simply cannot rationalize with a three-year-old, especially when it comes to taking medicines that do not taste good.

July 23, 2001 DAY +18

I had to leave Ben's side to go out into the hall, where I basically wanted to bang my head and fist against the wall. I was clenching my teeth, and I was angrier than I could ever remember being about anything.

I had taken more than I could handle. I kept trying to give Ben the medicines, but he would just sit in bed, look at me, and keep his lips tightly pursed. He shook his head "no" and would not budge. I held a spoonful of liquid in front of him for over fifty minutes, begging him to please just take it and wash it down with the juice that I had poured. He shook his head "no." I was mad and felt as if my blood were boiling. The angry emotion was so intense yet irrational. As much as I tried to reason with myself, I could not calm my feelings. I knew that this anger certainly was not going to help Ben take the medicine, so it was getting me nowhere. I had hoped by going out into the hall, by escaping from the four walls, by being away from the immediate situation, I was going to calm down a bit. Furthermore, I was going to be far away from Ben, whom I wanted to slug.

When I was out in the hall with my forehead pressed against the wall, I heard a muffled scream. I looked down the hall to my left, and there, about five doors down from ours, was another mother doing the exact same thing that I was doing. Our eyes met, and we both just started laughing and shaking our heads. Taking care of a sick child after transplant was not easy on anyone.

July 24, 2001 DAY +19

Ben's interests and activity proved to us that he was feeling a great deal better. He was sitting up and talking about wanting to eat. He was telling us about a variety of foods that he liked and was thinking out loud about what he wanted to eat first. He was truly showing some interest in food, and we were excited. It may seem like such a little thing to get excited about, but we felt as if we had just scaled the side of a mountain. The exhilaration of the conversation and sense of fulfillment was very satisfying and made us feel playful.

A Test of Faith

I wanted to run into the halls and shout out, "He's hungry!" but, of course, I had to control my enthusiastic mood.

"So, what would you like to eat?" I asked.

He thought for a moment and then replied, "I would like some pepperoni pizza, please."

I was shocked and asked, "Are you sure?" I thought that there was no way that his little tummy could manage something like pizza after all that it had gone through.

"Yes, pepperoni pizza sounds good," he said.

"Oh. Are you sure you wouldn't rather have a cup of chicken bouillon or maybe a saltine cracker? How about some red Jell-O?" I asked.

When he convinced me that pizza really was what he wanted to eat, I notified the nurse. She approved of the idea and said that some kids had come up with far worse choices than that over the years, so she said we should go for it. I agreed to the plan and told her that I would be off the floor for a few minutes and that Ben would be alone. She smiled and said good-bye to me. Then both she and Ben waved in unison as I left the room. Both of them had suspicious smiles on their faces, and I could hear giggling as the door closed behind me.

I bet that pretty little nurse could have gotten him to take his medicine.

I went down to the cafeteria, where a Domino's Pizza mini café was located. I explained to the man behind the counter that I needed him to make a fresh piece of pizza and explained the circumstances. When I was leaving the floor, the nurse had told me to remember that the rules still held true on Ben's food. Anything he was to eat must have been immediately prepared. Nothing could sit under a heat lamp, and this was to be a strict rule that we would need to pay attention to for at least the next six months.

The guy behind the counter did not show any sympathy. He actually was pretty rotten about it. I was an inconvenience to him, and he made it fairly clear that I was being a pain in his behind. I didn't care, though. I fixed myself a Diet Coke from the fountain machine. Standing against the back wall, I sipped my soda and did not move until my order was ready. When he finally handed over the slice of pepperoni pizza, I saw that the serving was presented on a plastic plate. I wrapped the entire plate with several layers of plastic wrap,

Sandie Klassen

paid him, and headed back upstairs. I hoped that Ben was serious and would eat at least one bite.

He did. He ate all of the cheese off the pizza and one piece of the pepperoni, and he licked the red tomato sauce off the crust. He did not want the crust, but who cared? HE ATE! This was such a great event.

Now we just had to get him to poop.

29

Home Away From Home

> July 25, 2001 DAY +20

Ben finally had a bowel movement! I was rejoicing when I heard him grunting, heard the expulsion of gas, and then heard the "release," but I was not prepared when I opened his diaper. It was probably the grossest thing that I had ever seen. His entire gastrointestinal tract had been so unbalanced and virtually nonfunctional for so long that the stool built up in him was a slimy, dark green, placenta-like gunk. I had to use nearly an entire box of baby wipes to clean him. It was a major disgusting blowout. I made some jokes about it to Ben, and we both sort of laughed as I wiped and wiped and wiped. I was actually glad and relieved that this mess was on the outside of him instead of the inside.

Although we were blessed with the fact that our health insurance policy had a "no limit" coverage clause, the hospital did not mess around when it was time for a patient to be discharged, and they completed the process as soon as possible. I believe that the insurance companies, with their managed-care health systems, somewhat dictated this activity, but, nevertheless, the hospital did not overextend their welcome to us.

"Since Ben is starting to eat, drink, and manage without the morphine, we feel he is about ready to be discharged from the unit," said the doctor during his morning rounds.

My mind started frantically searching for every reason why we were not ready to leave. It seemed as if there was a swarm of buzzing bees, each representing a different emotion, circling my head. At the same time, I felt as if my feet had been knocked out from under me, leaving me sitting, still in shock.

"Discharged? Are you kidding?" "We're only at Day Twenty, post transplant. We can't survive in the real world yet." "There are way too many germs out there!" "Please don't make us leave yet.

We're psychologically not ready." "No one ever gets out of here before at least thirty days, so it's way too early." "Shouldn't you reconsider this thought, doctor?" So many deliberations were hurrying through my mind! I asked the doctor every one of these questions and found myself begging to be allowed to stay, at least for a little longer. We truly weren't ready—were we?

The doctor chuckled, but I didn't think my concerns were all that funny. He calmed my onrush of panic by explaining that we had a tremendous amount of work to do before we could actually be released, but the plan was to begin the teaching, send in the social worker and the discharge coordinator, set up for a home health nurse to come to the apartment, meet with the pharmacist who would supply all of the home medication needs, and, basically, get our mind-set right. Yes, it was going to be a whole new world out there, and we had to understand it. We had to learn and completely comprehend our new responsibilities for Ben's continued safety and protection.

July 26, 2001 DAY +21

The pharmacist was the first to arrive for our discharge education sessions.

"Can't you possibly make this medicine taste any better?" I asked.

She giggled.

I said, "I'm totally serious. I cannot fight with this child for two hours every morning and two hours every night to get him to swallow one teaspoonful of this syrup, and then have to work on the seventeen other pills. Please try to come up with something," I pleaded and almost demanded.

She said she'd try, and if it worked, she would patent it. I wished her good luck and really and truly hoped that she could come up with something.

I was really scared to even think about going back into the real world. Things on the unit were so protected, and we had mastered a system of coping with Ben's needs. Also, we had help. Professional help. At the apartment, it was going to be us on our own. Me, actually. Chuck was not good with the idea of giving Ben shots, hooking up lines to his garden hoses, doing dressing changes, giving medicines, and, believe it or not, drawing blood. We were told that we were going to have to draw blood from Ben every morning so that it could be dropped off at the lab. By the time the lab processed it, the results would be in the hands of the doctor by around 10:00 a.m., the time at which Ben was to see the doctor every single day, seven days a week.

In addition to the above responsibilities, we were also going to have to continue Ben on the IV feeding (TPN) program at the apartment. He would have to be hooked up to this feeding system for twelve hours every night. This was going to be a necessary requirement of us at home until his weight climbed to a safe level, which would then be some indication that he was receiving adequate nourishment. They could not afford for him to get into a position of malnutrition or dehydration. At this time, he was at too much risk for such a state, so the TPN was the best safety precaution and solution. With the damage done to his digestive system by the mucositis, the process of absorption of vitamins and minerals through the small intestine was poor. His body was going to need some help to grow stronger and healthier, and this help was going to come in the form of the TPN.

With all of this news of my upcoming responsibilities, major ones at that, I was more than overwhelmed. I collapsed into the chair in Ben's room and just sat with my hands folded in my lap. I didn't know if I was capable of handling all of the nursing duties coming my way. I didn't think I was going to be able to do all of this. I was afraid that I was going to hurt Ben by doing something wrong. I needed a tremendous amount of education, and I needed a lot of time to study all of my new duties before I would feel comfortable taking on these tasks.

July 27, 2001 DAY +22

Chuck stayed at Ben's bedside while Miss Patty and I did a job on the apartment. We scoured every corner of the place with about every cleaner we could find on the grocery store shelf. We used Lysol, bleach, Soft Scrub, Pine-Sol, and bleach wipes. We changed the shower curtains to new ones and went to the office to ask about more carpet cleaning. I was sure by this point that the girls in the apartment complex office were thinking that we were paranoid, and we were.

We continued our cleaning frenzy with the outside windows, door, screened area, and entryway, and we did not neglect the air conditioner filters. They were cleaned to perfection as well. The place was spotless, speckless, and, most definitely, germ free—and it had to remain that way.

It felt so good to be done with our job. We sat on the couch, looked around, and admired our work. The place looked great. We were at least physically ready for Ben to come home.

July 28, 2001 DAY +23

The intensive training to prepare for Ben's discharge continued at his bedside. The home health nurse came in to explain the time-consuming and delicate procedure of hooking up the TPN feeding system. She spent two hours teaching me about the two pumps and the two different types of fluids that would be attached to them and to Benjamin. She explained about the injection of the multivitamin into the main fluid bag, the other medicines that would be injected into Ben, and the pump settings that would be optimal to push the TPN. She told me about the exact temperatures at which everything had to be stored and then explained how to warm the fluids to the proper temperature so that they could be safely administered into Ben's body.

She reviewed the flushing procedures of the central lines and the techniques of changing the caps so that I could do this once per day. If the cap at the end of the garden hose was not changed at exactly the right time, the sugars from the TPN solutions could produce some sort of growth that could potentially get into Ben and cause him great harm.

She reviewed the procedure for the dressing changes and explained the necessity of preciseness in all of my actions to further prevent infection in Ben's still immune-deficit body. She spoke rapidly, technically, and non-stop, hardly pausing to take a breath, for the full duration of her time in Ben's room. Then she turned to me and had the nerve to ask, "So, do you have all that?"

I looked at her with a perplexed expression and replied with great hesitation, "Not really. There sure is a lot to do, and I need to see the process of setting the TPN pumps at least one more time. I think I can still do all of the cap and dressing change work," I told her.

I really needed to hear her explanation about the TPN one hundred more times, but I did not want her to feel bad because I was only able to absorb about one-tenth of all that she had said. I felt as if my brain had turned to mush and that I needed each and every step typed out for me. The details were so critical to Ben's health and safety that I could not afford to miss even the smallest detail. I could never live with myself if I made a mistake that ultimately hurt him.

Because of the massive amount of information that we were required to process, and because of the seriousness of the matter for Ben's sake, we were able to get approval from the doctor and the insurance company to have the nurse come to the apartment for "a few" visits to help set up the TPN in the evening and then to disconnect everything in the morning. It actually took about eight days of the nurse's visits before I felt completely comfortable in all that I had to do! I was probably ok to take care of things on my own after five days, but I liked the nurse very well and so did Ben. Her visits were a welcome relief from what was otherwise a ban from contact with other humans and the outside world. But, after the eight days, sixteen total visits, I really did feel one hundred percent comfortable and confident that I wouldn't mess up the procedure. Actually, I guess you could say that I felt ninety-five percent comfortable. I still had a healthy sense of fear, which was good. It kept me moving and working with slow and methodical care.

The TPN duties were a nightmare for me. I would wake up hours before dawn and start thinking about the process of disconnecting the hoses. I reviewed the order of the steps in my mind over and over again to be reassured that I had everything right.

I was so happy and relieved after three weeks when the doctor finally said, "No more TPN." Those were the greatest words to hear. I felt as if a ton of bricks had been lifted off my shoulders.

July 29, 2001 DAY +24

When the discharge coordinator came into our transplant room about 1:00 p.m., she had a stack of papers to review with us and many signature requirements. When we finished learning about all of the dos and don'ts for our new life, the nurse assigned to our discharge turned to us and said simply, "Congratulations." The words were ringing in my ears for days. I loved the successful sound of the word "congratulations." I felt relieved and happy, satisfied, and downright lucky.

Miss Patty, Lisa, and Dana came to the unit so that we could all enjoy the well-earned "confetti party" and celebration together. The time for us to leave the transplant unit and take Ben back to the apartment had come. We'd made it! After a total of thirty-five days in isolation, we'd finally made it. We were being discharged from the bone marrow transplant unit at Duke University, and we were celebrating a successful autologous transplant. We did it, Ben did it, Jesus did it, and it was reason to celebrate.

Chuck had already taken our now disheveled under-the-bed storage box and the suitcase of toys, games, and books down to the car. The window on the door looked so bare since I had taken down the pictures and Ben's name earlier that morning. The room was white, sterile, and drab. There was no color and no life left in it, but it did not bother me. I was ready to leave this modern-day plastic bubble, and I was ready for us to be together as a family back in our apartment, our home away from home.

I opened the door to Ben's room and held it open for the first time in over a month. Before this time, the door had to be opened as slightly as possible so that the person coming in or out could just barely squeeze through it. The door was not to be held open for any length of time and certainly never to be propped open. But now, without any hesitation, I held the door wide open so that we could all walk out into the hallway.

We carefully took our positions in the hallway and prepared our cameras for pictures. Ben was going to be the last to leave the room. When it was time for our son to come out, my heart was pounding and my eyes were teary. Our skinny little boy, dressed in shorts and a collared shirt, socks, gym shoes, and a green surgical mask, slowly made his way out of the room to join us. The entire nursing staff and two of the doctors stood with us in the hallway. All of us at the same time yelled, "Hooray, Ben!" and we threw confetti on him. He smiled and tried to reach up to catch some of the shredded, colored, construction paper pieces. He had paper on the top of his head and all over his shirt. One little yellow piece stuck on his eyelash. We all laughed, cheered, and clapped. Then we left the unit. We were on our way home.

Chuck drove like he did the very first time we brought Ben and then Dana home from the hospital when they were first born. His driving was slow, cautious, and safer than I had ever seen before. Just like that day, nearly four years ago, after Ben's birth, now, too, we were bringing home a brand new life.

30

Rainbows

Ben was home!!! For the first time in thirty-three days, the four of us were spending the evening and sleeping under the same roof together as a family. We felt as if we had been given the gift of a new beginning.

Ben and Dana hugged and played lovingly together, while Chuck and I simply admired our priceless children. They truly were our gifts from God. We felt so lucky.

We had a tremendous amount of work to do once we were out of the hospital. For another thirty-four days, we stayed in Durham so that we could go to the day clinic. The day clinic was called "Rainbow Day," and we were expected to be there every morning for Ben to have a physical examination. We also had a meeting with a doctor and received the report on the morning's blood work.

Our first stop each day was to visit Miss Karlene, who would measure Ben's vital signs, height, and weight. Ben loved Miss Karlene and I did, too. She made us feel so warm and welcome in the otherwise huge and strictly business medical system. As a thank-you gift for her friendliness to us, Ben gave her a stuffed animal, the Donkey from the movie *Shrek*. When you squeezed the donkey's chest, he said, "Man, I like you! What's your name?" Ben and Miss Karlene greeted each other every day with this lighthearted locution. It was a perfect start to each of our Rainbow Day visits.

We had a lot of ups and downs during this time as we had to deal with positive blood cultures indicating bacteria in Ben's hoses, changes and adjustments in medications, a few follow-up scans and tests, and other minor but manageable complications. Going to Rainbow Day was always a long ordeal. Sometimes Ben would receive blood transfusions of either packed red cells or platelets, sometimes he would receive long doses of IV medications, and sometimes he would just get a pat on the back, a big smile, and a "See

A Test of Faith

you tomorrow, kiddo" from the doctor. As you can imagine, we really liked those days.

Ben wore his mask without any trouble and didn't mind that I had him washing his hands a zillion times a day. He still fought with me every morning about taking his medicines and again each night. He was not fond of the IV night feedings, either, because he was just plain tired of being hooked up to what seemed to be miles of plastic tubing and a pole all night long, but he managed well enough. The IV feedings at the apartment lasted a total of three weeks, and then he was finally able to be free from the plastic tubing leash and the beeping pumps at night. On the first night of freedom, he rolled around in bed, back and forth, over and over, until he was completely rolled up in his blankets like a burrito. We laughed and celebrated as he made an entire mess of the blankets and sheets on his bed.

The biggest celebration was when his central line was finally removed on the last day of August. The port would have to stay in for a least another year, but that was fine with us. With the central line gone, Ben was going to be able to eventually take a normal bath and go swimming. We just had to wait for the surgical site to close up and completely heal. It had been way too long already for Ben to have to watch from the sidelines. Sitting at the side of the pool and watching the other children swim was nothing but torture for him. He always insisted on being there, though. He wanted to watch Dana learn to float on her back, and he wanted to cheer her on.

Every day that passed, Ben got stronger. He smiled more, played harder, did not complain of pain, laughed a lot, and began to show more and more interest in eating. His weight was gaining nicely, and his blood chemistry studies indicated that there was some pretty decent absorption of the foods he was eating. He soon developed enough strength in his legs to climb up a step without assistance. His liver and kidneys were recovering from their traumatic experience and so were his mouth and digestive tract.

His shiny bald head began to grow some peach fuzz, and we all loved to rub our hands on it. He was so proud of his new hair that he would ask us often to feel the growth. "Look Daddy, I'm getting some hair," or "Feel this, Mommy," he would say with excitement.

On one of our last days at Duke before we were to go home to Florida, we had to wait hours to see the doctor. Things in the clinic were crazy that day, and it was already very late in the afternoon. The sun had lost its intensity and shadows were being cast through the window of the isolation waiting room. A family that we had not met before sat on the couch across from us. We were all tired and hungry and sitting very quietly. Everyone seemed to be studying his or her own thoughts until someone broke the silence. I cannot remember how the conversation started, but I do remember vividly how it ended. The family seemed very nervous and withdrawn, and when they finally spoke, the father explained that they were preparing for admission to the bone marrow transplant unit and they were scared to death.

Their six-year-old son was a handsome boy with large, dark brown eyes that were bright, healthy-looking, and beautiful. They were the very dark brown that blended with the pupil so that you could not determine where the pupil ended and the iris started. His eyes looked like perfect marbles, and they immediately drew you in. They expressed love and innocence. Ben was sitting across from the small, bald-headed boy in this waiting room when the other boy spoke first.

"Was it scary?" he asked Ben.

Chuck and I and the other two parents sat stunned for a moment. We spoke not a word while we waited for Ben's answer.

After what seemed like a very long silence, Ben finally looked into the eyes of the slightly taller boy. Speaking firmly but compassionately, Ben replied as if he were an experienced professional on the topic. He spoke in a matter-of-fact but very loving tone when he said, "Don't be scared, little boy. Jesus will hold your hand, and He will make you all better. He will protect you just like He did me."

The room grew silent again. The power of Ben's words needed nothing but stillness to really sink in. The words were spoken from the innocent heart of a three-year-old boy to that of a scared six-year-old. The conversation was somehow far too mature for such little people, yet at the same time, the brief conversation was much more profound than any adult could have ever made it. It moved me beyond words. Ben was not at all afraid to tell someone what he thought about Jesus. He had shared a complete, uninhibited thought with his new friend.

Suddenly, I was looking at the world through the eyes of this child, and I was changed. That conversation, those words Ben spoke, refreshed me of the promise I had read over and over again in my Bible. I felt a renewed sense of security and a purpose in life that I will hold on to forever.

31

Going In Style

Chuck spent most of the morning at the kitchen table searching through the yellow pages while I did the last-minute cleaning of the apartment and applied the finishing touches to the packing. I had to bother Chuck twice to get his assistance on the overstuffed suitcases; I needed him to sit on the bags so that I could get them zippered shut. I have no idea how we accumulated so many additional things in Durham, but we did. We had more boxes of toys and stuffed animals and even more clothes than when we started this journey, and somehow, it all had to make it back to Florida in the same two vehicles that had brought it all here. The floor space near the front door of the apartment was stacked high with full cardboard boxes, suitcases, car seats, strollers, and everything else that was to be loaded up for the trip home.

Lisa had flown back to Ft. Myers a couple of weeks earlier so that she would have time to shop for school clothes, spend some time with her dad and girlfriends, and get settled at home, all before she started the eighth grade.

Miss Patty was enjoying her time alone in her apartment and spent several hours reading, writing letters, and meditating with her Bible. The summer's experience had somehow changed all of our perspectives on life, and it was not unusual for any one of us to be found reading from a Bible or searching our souls. We hadn't turned into fanatics, but we certainly felt the power of the scriptures of the Holy Bible and were seeking answers to what our real purposes in life were. We were trying to figure out what special plan God had in mind for us so that we could live it out. This summer taught us that nothing in life should be taken for granted, as the time we are given here on earth is short and fragile, yet extremely significant. What we make of this time is up to us.

A Test of Faith

I feel sometimes as if this world is a giant quilt, and we are all looking up at the underside of the stitching. It is plain, white fabric and reveals nothing. Each of us sews our threads as we make our choices, live our lives, and react to the obstacles and heartaches that come our way. I feel sometimes that the stitching is terribly chaotic and that there is a complete absence of order. It seems that the places where we are sometimes forced to make our stitches are dreadfully unfair, and at times, they make no sense at all. Someday, however, when we get to heaven, we will have the opportunity to look down at the topside of this quilt, and then we will see the magnificent and beautiful pattern and design that we all made together. We will see how and why we all interacted and why things happened as they did. We will finally see the perfect piece of work that God has been tending to for so long. We all do make tremendous contributions to this quilt and to this world, and we need to accept and honor those contributions.

Rodney was scheduled to leave Ft. Myers about the time that Chuck had all of his weight on my second suitcase. By the time I had the apartment completely organized, Rod would be descending into Raleigh-Durham International Airport (RDU), located about twenty-five miles from our apartment. Chuck had plans to travel past the famous Research Triangle area of this prestigious, scientific medical community to pick up his travel companion, while I would call in one last order from our favorite Chinese restaurant, the very same place that we discovered on the day of our arrival in this city of Durham, otherwise known as the "City of Medicine."

When the men returned from the airport, Chuck, Rodney, Patty, and I loaded up both cars, while Ben and Dana helped by carrying out the light pillows, blankets, and favorite stuffed animals for their journey to our real home in the Sunshine State. Before sunset, we had both cars completely jam-packed. The sport utility vehicles were both so stuffed that each and every free space in the cargo area, back seat, and passenger seats was occupied by something. There were even shoes stashed onto the dashboard in the far right corner of Chuck's windshield. We completed our work as early as possible so that after dinner, the two men would theoretically be well rested, well fed, and energized for their long drive south at daybreak.

The search through the phone book's yellow pages proved to be successful. After making several calls and inquiries, Chuck was finally able to settle on a company that could fit the bill. He made the reservation. The shiny, stretch limousine was to arrive at Deerfield Apartments at 10:00 a.m., and the driver would take Miss Patty, Dana, Ben, and me to the airport. We had to celebrate going home, and a taxi was just not going to cut it this time. Chuck explained my plan to the owner of the limousine company over the phone, and I noticed that he was smiling widely as he listened to her promise to help make the event as special as possible.

When the long car made its way into the apartment complex's parking lot, the four of us were already standing on the sidewalk. The day was perfect. The sky was a bright blue, and there were only a few puffy white clouds off in the distance. The temperature was warm but comfortable, and the air was fragrant from the summer flowers. When the limousine stopped in front of us, I admired it from front to back. The corners were rounded and contoured magnificently, and the luster and sheen of the paint was flawless. It was brand new and elegant. The polished, black Lincoln had a camel leather interior and room for at least six adults.

Miss Charlie, the driver, was dressed in a white shirt with a black tie, black tuxedo jacket, and matching black skirt. Most importantly, she had a warm, grandmotherly smile. When Miss Charlie opened the back door for us, Ben crawled in first. To his surprise and delight, there, tied to the center table, was a silver and red Mylar Elmo balloon. Dana was equally surprised and happy with our guest passenger.

When our bags were loaded into the trunk, Miss Charlie asked if we were ready to head to the airport. I asked if we could first take a short detour.

She gracefully and slowly drove the automobile into the horseshoe drive and up to the front door of the Duke University Medical Center. All eyes seemed to turn to look as we came to a complete stop. Miss Charlie made her way around the car to open the back passenger door while I filled the champagne glasses with Seven-Up from the mini bar. When we all had our glasses ready, we crawled out of the car to stand beside each other. Several people stopped to see what was happening, and it took all of the self-control I could muster not to yell out something like, "We made it!" or "The cancer is gone!" or "We did it!" or "Praise God!" or "Thank You everyone for all of your help!" Most of all, I wanted to shout, "Thank you, God, from the bottom of my heart, that I am taking my baby home." I wanted to share my bursting joy with everyone, but I didn't. I just smiled and put my arm around Ben.

As we stood beside the limousine at the medical center's front door, Miss Charlie included, we toasted the hospital and the heavens, and we said thank you. The medical center's valet took a picture of us as we clinked our glasses.

Epilogue

We are now one full year post-transplant, and Benjamin remains in complete remission. Our lives have been completely changed by this experience, and it has been a positive change. After Ben was diagnosed with cancer, we realized what the important things in life really were. We learned that good health is very delicate, and we should treasure it and be thankful for it. We learned that every day that we wake up healthy is a gift from God. We learned that material things, such as cars, houses, money, clothes, and a fully stamped passport, play no role in a person's true happiness. A relationship of love with family, friends, neighbors, strangers, and God is all that we really need to have peace and fulfillment.

We learned that no one knows when the time will come to be called to die. You could be three years old, twenty years old or one hundred years old. When you die, obviously, the chance you had to know and serve your Lord is gone.

In my opinion, there are only two things in this life that really matter. The first is to know in your heart if you have a relationship with Jesus Christ and if you have accepted Him as your savior. This alone will ensure your place in Heaven and your eternal life. I believe the second thing that really matters in this life is how you treat other people. I do not care if they are rich or poor, fat or thin, clean or dirty, successful or derelict. They are people who have the exact same needs and desires as you and I, and they should all be treated with love and respect. No one person is any better than another. Cancer does not single out anyone or any particular class of people, and neither should we.

I have been asked to speak to more groups than I can count about my experience as a caregiver for someone with cancer. When I share my story, I learn over and over again the surprising truth that cancer essentially gives people back their lives. In many ways, as strange as it seems, cancer is a gift. People living selfishly or without thought of what comes after death have told me that cancer was the jolt that made them sit back and think about their true purpose in life. As a result, they got back on track. Family members of those who did not survive their battles with this horrible disease have told me that their relatives died better people because they had a chance to reflect on who they were, what they did, and where they wanted to spend eternity.

I have been asked to interview for numerous television news segments and newspaper articles, and I was invited to serve as an honorary chair for a cancer fund-raising event. In all of this, I learned that people are lonely and afraid, and when someone offers a loving touch or a kind word, it is often enough to reinvigorate them to continue their fight against the disease, or to succumb to it peacefully.

I have also been invited to speak on the gift of donating blood. I learned that people are afraid of the needle, but when they overcome that fear, they have more satisfaction than they ever dreamed possible because they knew that they might have just saved the life of a small child.

When I stand in front of all of these people, I somehow want to express to them that we could not have fought this cancer alone, and I want to thank them for their love and support during this time in our lives. I want to go into the crowd and hug each and every person and tell them how important they are, how valuable their lives are, and how much they really do make a difference in this world. Even though most are strangers, I want to tell them how much of a difference they made in our lives and Ben's. I want them to know that they unknowingly were caregivers to someone with cancer. When they offered even the least bit of compassion, they helped. They helped because they gave the sick person—or in my case, the parent—hope. Without coming on too strongly, I want to somehow tell them that Jesus Christ is who He says He is, and it doesn't have to take something tragic like cancer to get to know Him. If you trust in your faith, you will honestly and truly experience His love for you. You will see and feel miraculous events in your life. It is really almost too powerful to tell about.

People whom I do not even know come up to me in the grocery store and tell me how Benjamin has been their inspiration and how their outlook on life has become more positive because of him. They tell me that they know of his story because of the fantastic and heartwarming newspaper articles written by the same award-winning writer that I mentioned earlier. They tell me that they no longer feel sorry for themselves, but rather are uplifted and have a renewed passion for life.

So many people live their lives at a hectic pace, with stresses that overpower any chance of experiencing tranquility and happiness. They forget to look at the blue sky or feel the warm air, and they certainly forget to enjoy the children when they are young, innocent, and so loving. They neglect to hold on to and enjoy the precious moment called life. I am glad that Ben's cancer has made so many people reflect on who they are and how they are living. It pleases me that God used this horrendous experience to inspire and change so many people.

Chuck ran the San Diego Marathon, all 26.2 miles, in honor of Benjamin at the ten-month anniversary of his transplant. He ran in a T-shirt with a picture of his son on the back and the words, "I'm Running for Ben." He said that his purpose was to help all adults and children with cancer to find a cure in any way possible.

He ran the race with the Leukemia and Lymphoma Society Team-In-Training Program, and he alone raised a national record of $24,020.00 for cancer research and patient services. He wrote a letter telling Ben's story and mailed it out to everyone in his Rolodex. He does not know exactly how many letters he mailed, but 262 people sent money and personal notes back to him, sponsoring him in the race. Many of the letters he received included stories of mothers, sisters, or friends who had battled cancer. Chuck figured that no matter how much pain and suffering he had to endure while running the race, it was nothing compared to what Benjamin and all cancer victims faced every day.

When Chuck crossed the finish line, a race attendant noticed Ben's picture on the shirt and asked, "So, you're running for this little boy. Do you know him?"

Chuck replied, "Yes, he's my son."

The attendant asked if Ben was still alive, and Chuck said, "YES!!"

She proceeded to put a medal around Chuck's neck and then handed him a second large gold medal. "Please give this to your son," she said. "He's winning the most important race of all. He's winning the battle against cancer."

We continue to visit Dr. Salman, M.D.; Miss Debbie, our nurse; and Dr. Salman's new partner, Dr. MacArthur, M.D., Ph.D., every three weeks for blood work. We go to Duke's Children's Hospital every three months for a complete workup.

We are so thankful that Dr. MacArthur has come on staff with Dr. Salman. Believe it or not, Dr. MacArthur is a neuroblastoma specialist, and he has a tremendous amount of experience with the disease. He was trained at the very prestigious Washington University School of Medicine in St. Louis, Missouri, and has made extraordinary accomplishments in his young career. The man is only forty-three years old, yet he has already published over twenty-four manuscripts and technical papers and lectured over one hundred times on clinical and scientific matters. He holds numerous appointments locally and nationally, and he's experienced with all levels of neuroblastoma and childhood cancer. He is also incredibly lovable, which makes him perfectly suited for Dr. Salman's team. Having such an expert helping to care for our son right here in Ft. Myers, Florida, is just another example of the fact that our dreams and prayers do come true.

Our fight with this cancer is not yet over, and I admit that I am still very scared of a recurrence. I worry about Ben often but try not to let my fears get out of control and rule my life. When I find myself overwhelmed, I simply pray out loud Psalm 91 in the name of Jesus: *"No harm shall come near (Ben); No plague (cancer) shall overtake (Ben)"* (Psalm 91:10). I trust that God hears my prayer. There must be no sign of the cancer for five years before the doctors will declare Ben cured, and I trust that we will make it.

Ben is a happy, healthy, outgoing boy, and he's very smart, too. He remembers everything that has happened over the past two years and often refers back to when he had his "bad cell." This little boy is my inspiration. He has been so brave and heroic, yet so innocent throughout the whole fight. At just three years old, he was asked to fight for his life. He didn't know exactly what was happening, and he didn't realize the tremendous odds that were put against him, so he took on the challenge and won.

Ben has taught me to slow down and enjoy the time that passes so quickly. He sees the world through the eyes of a child, and he lives for the moment. He does not judge or criticize or complain; he just loves and enjoys everyone he meets and everything he does. He trusts God. He has taught me that we, too, should embrace this attitude.

Sandie Klassen

I pray that our story brings you hope and peace in this moment and many joyful moments to come. May God bless you and your family.

About the Author

Sandie Klassen owns Bonita Springs Sports and Physical Therapy Center. She is an energetic physical therapist and businesswoman. She enjoys public speaking related to physical therapy and cancer caregiving.

Her education includes a B.S. in Kinesiology, a M.S. in Exercise Physiology, and an additional M.S. in Physical Therapy.

She is active in her community and church. Her most important job, and the one she loves best, is "Mom" to Ben and Dana.

Printed in the United States
24513LVS00003B/235-282